I0062028

VETERANS IN FRANCHISING

THE UNOFFICIAL GUIDE FOR U.S. MILITARY
VETERANS SEEKING INFORMATION ON
FRANCHISE OPPORTUNITIES

JACK CHILD

Copyright © 2025 by Jack Child

Veterans in Franchising: The Unofficial Guide for U.S. Military Veterans Seeking Information on Franchise Opportunities
Book@VeteranServiceBrands.com

Published 2025, by Veteran Service Brands
VeteransInFranchising.com

Print ISBN: 979-8218666309
Epub ISBN: 979-8218666316
Library of Congress Control Number: 2025908132

All rights reserved.

No part of this book may be reproduced in any form or by any electronic or mechanical means, including information storage and retrieval systems, without written permission from the author, except for the use of brief quotations in a book review.

While I used AI and ChatGPT to assist with research,
I'm proud to report no wording in this book is the product of any
artificial intelligence aids.
Jack Child

CONTENTS

Introduction

When you hear the word "franchise," what comes to mind? Typically McDonald's®, Dunkin'®, Subway®, KFC®, Burger King®, Dairy Queen®, Taco Bell®, etc.

Franchising is big business.

But it's also very big small business!

That AAMCO® Transmission Center in town? It's a franchise likely owned by a neighbor whose kids go to the same school as yours. The Mosquito Joe® you hired to kill mosquitoes in your back yard is a locally owned franchise. Maybe you hired Monster® Tree Service to clear some fallen limbs and shape that maple tree you desperately want to keep. Yep, it's a franchise, too, and the owner is another local. Even brands like McDonald's are most often locally owned and operated.

The world of franchising is much more than big name brands, and owning a franchise is so much more accessible than most realize. I'm writing this Field Manual to help my fellow veterans better understand the opportunities (and potential pitfalls) of owning a franchise and maybe open a few doors they might not know exist.

If you're tired of working for "the man," or feeling under-appreciated at work, or dismayed seeing others benefit from your efforts more than you, then this Field Manual is for you.

Conversely, say you are appreciated at work and you're making a good living, but something is calling you to strike out on your own entrepreneurial journey. This Field Manual is for you.

Maybe you already own a solo entrepreneurial business, but you feel like you can't keep up with marketing, software, skills, etc., and there's a franchise brand you'll have to compete against that's marching its way to you. Yes, you guessed it: This Field Manual is for you.

Let's say you're that E-7/E-8/E-9 or a Mustang O-4 or O-5 about to retire. The military is all you've ever known. You thought by now you'd land that sweet consulting gig. You're not getting the interviews you want. Or, maybe you just can't see yourself behind a desk working for someone else, but you aren't certain as to what's next. Perhaps this Field Manual can help you find your next chapter.

Finally, perhaps you're a veteran who's already in the franchise space and you feel like there's more to learn. Maybe you're struggling with your own franchise, or everything is fine, but you'd like to branch out and build your empire. I think you'll find some valuable pieces of information in here to make reading this Field Manual well worth your while as well.

But, before we get into the business at hand of telling you all the wonderful, "sunshine and roses" stories about the world of franchising (salted with a few not so great ones), a little background is in order, so you have a frame of reference for what I'm about to share.

A reminder: Putting aside the next few paragraphs, this book really isn't about me. Promise. It's about you. My editor forced me to give you some of my background to set the stage for this manual.

Blame him.

Here we go . . .

About Me

Let me open with this. Much of what I've found most rewarding in my life (outside of family) flows directly from my decision to enlist in the Army: three years of challenging assignments with outsized responsibilities, the ability to attend college on the G.I. Bill, ROTC, and eventual selection for Air Force Pilot Training.

The military afforded me the opportunity to work undercover as a Military Police Investigator on the CID/MPI Drug Team, made it possible for me to try my hand at fingertip and four ship formations, fly inverted, pull eight Gs, and go faster than the speed of sound (frowned upon to do all of these at the same time), fly into a combat zone on my very first mission alongside a "crusty old" lieutenant colonel (he was probably 45), serve as C-141 aircraft commander and instructor pilot, fly as far north as Thule, Greenland, as far south as Johannesburg, as far west as Japan and Korea, as far east as the Middle East, and countless places in between.

My last job in the Air Force was to teach new aircraft commanders how to get gas (and not hit the tanker).

A view from the refueling boom control station aboard a 452nd Air Refueling Wing KC-135 Stratotanker as a C-141B Starlifter aircraft refuels in flight over Altus Air Force Base. Both aircraft are manned by Air Force Reserve crews. (NARA & DVIDS Public Domain Archive)

Post-service, I stepped out of one cockpit and right into another one 10 days later as a Delta® Air Lines Second Officer. Upgraded to First Officer after two years. Then, Captain nine years later.

My income as a Delta pilot allowed me to pursue my entrepreneurial dreams, which is where my real passion lies.

How did this dumb, white, Irish kid from the South Side of Chicago (what my high school friend Barney Brannigan called guys like us) get to be an Airbus A350 Captain at Delta and, later, a franchisor? It all starts with the decision to walk into the Army recruiter's office two blocks down from the Gas City where I used to pump gas with Barney during my high school years. By the way, Barney went on to become a wildly successful commodities trader at the Chicago Mercantile Exchange. Rest in peace, my friend.

For many years I tended to reduce my Air Force experience to one where I mostly just learned to fly. I've now come to realize the military taught me so much more than that. I was capable of more things than I ever dreamed possible. I'm fairly certain that, upon your own reflection, you might feel the same way, no matter what assignments you had.

The very high standards by which we flew at Delta, along with Delta's status as the standard-bearer for U.S. carriers, also provided invaluable lessons directly translatable to franchising. (insert groan from my buddies at other airlines)

That moment you know you've arrived

With benefit of hindsight, I've come to more deeply appreciate my privilege to serve in the military and in a follow-on career structured very much like the military. Now, I consider it my privilege (and obligation) to share some of what I've learned with my fellow veterans about the opportunities and potential traps for Veterans in Franchising.

Why Listen to Me

First of all, you don't have to.

Skepticism towards people who make claims about what you should or shouldn't do, or how to approach a given task, or what franchise to buy, is healthy. It goes a long way toward maintaining balance.

However, I'm sure you've also come across colleagues, authors, podcasters, and the like who have resonated with you because you connected with them at some level, you trusted in their expertise, or they struck you as being straight shooters with no particular axe to grind.

This book is written to be direct and avoid much of the fluff and platitudes you'll find in other franchise how-to books. As Viper says to Maverick, "I'm not gonna sit here and blow sunshine up your ass, Lieutenant."

Full disclosure: I also have some axes to grind.

The following are some of my beefs.

I get frustrated seeing veterans struggle in civilian life. I get frustrated knowing there are so many opportunities unique to veterans that most are just simply unaware of. And I get particularly frustrated seeing veterans being taken advantage of in the business world. Certain excerpts in this book are the grinding of said axes.

My Franchise Background

In 2005 I started a local driveway sealcoating business that quickly took off, using strong branding, highly effective marketing, and a focus on fierce customer service.

I franchised the concept in 2006 and sold about a dozen franchises over the next few years. I then launched the very first parking lot striping franchise concept in 2009—and was swiftly mocked for attempting to franchise such a thing. *Who needs a franchise for that? Anybody can do it!* There are now five franchise brands in that space. I was just a bit ahead of my time.

I took on a partner in 2010 and things were just starting to take off when he got entangled in a lawsuit that was separate, but tangentially related to the franchise. This created havoc within the franchise, and I decided it would be best to part ways and sell the business in 2012. As part of the sale, I signed a five-year non-compete agreement.

By this time, my partner had fallen completely off the face of the earth and the plaintiff decided to come after me. After two years in federal court and countless sleepless nights, the case was finally dismissed in 2014 in my favor.

WARNING

Choose your business partners wisely.

Illegitimi Non Carborundum

With all the pain and loss of that experience, I never imagined I'd go back into that industry. But my initial instincts were still correct—the market remained yearning for a national pavement marking brand. None existed in 2017.

I decided I needed to trust my instincts and not let the bastards grind me down.

One of the most important lessons I learned during all this was the veterans in my former brands were the easiest to work with. We understood each other and the importance of teamwork in a way that I just couldn't get across to many of the non-veteran franchisees. I also felt certain the pavement marking business would be a great first business for veterans to own and operate.

How could I increase the number of veterans on our team? By becoming the very first franchise brand to offer franchises exclusively to veterans. You can't own one unless you're a vet.

G-FORCE® Franchises for Veterans and G-FORCE® Parking Lot Striping were born.

I really had a particular motivation to assist post 9/11 veterans who had it so much worse than my own military experience. No one ever did the "Thank you for your service" bit with me until a few years after 9/11. It never dawned on me prior to this that anyone should feel obligated to say thank you. I realized they were really thanking me for others' more recent sacrifices (yes, I know, we all served, but the post

9/11 folks went through so much more than my generation and my own personal experiences).

Maybe helping to set them up for success in a business would be my small way of giving back. Full disclosure: I'm not running a charity. We expect to make money after our franchisees make money.

We sold our first G-FORCE Parking Lot Striping franchise in 2018 to an Iraq War veteran and, as of this writing in 2025, we now stand at 50 locations.

G-FORCE was listed as a Top 50 Contractor by *Pavement Maintenance® Magazine* for 2023 and 2024, one of the Top 500 Franchises by *Entrepreneur® Magazine* in 2023, a 2024 Top Franchise for Diversity, Equity, and Inclusion, and ranked #61 for *Entrepreneur Magazine*'s Top Low Cost Franchises for 2024.[1]

In 2022, I co-founded Veteran Service Brands™ (VSB) with my close friend and business partner, Craig Laquerre, a franchisee from one of my earlier brands. VSB is a franchise umbrella organization offering four different franchise opportunities exclusively to veterans: G-FORCE, PAINT CORPS® Commercial and Residential Painting, MACH ONE® Epoxy Floors, and FIELD OPS® Athletic Field and Game Court Markings.

VSB now has almost 100 locations with a nationwide reach. We are the largest veteran-only franchise organization of its kind, and we are building the largest veteran-owned service network in the country.

VSB has plans to add three more franchised service brands and grow to 500 locations over the next 10 years.

VSB franchise partners and corporate staff have over 1,000 years of combined military service as of this writing. Ten centuries of service! That number humbles me.

Those are the facts, but still I don't think that is enough reason for you to listen to what I have to say.

Maybe this is:

I'm not selling you anything. I'm not trying to sell you a franchise. I'm not asking you to be part of any of our companies. I'm not trying to convince you one way or the other that franchising is right for you.

Neither am I offering you legal advice or saying you must do A or B.

What I am offering is a front row seat, so you know how the franchise sausage is made. This is the book I wish I had 25 years ago. Much of what is in this book is hard won. Intelligence without experience can be a terrible handicap: You think you know, but you don't. That leads to wasted time, energy, and money. I want this book to be something you can use to save on all three of those precious commodities.

Not everyone who picks up this book will decide to join a franchise. The goal isn't to convince you to do anything but to help guide your research and encourage you to look within to make sure this is the right move for you. If you decide franchising is not for you after reading this book, then that's a win for both of us because it means you took the time to investigate, to double-check, and then decide. And, if I helped you come to that conclusion, that's a win for me as well. Owning a franchise is not for everyone.

So, as Forrest Gump, a fellow Army veteran, once famously said, "That's all I have to say about that!" ("that" being me).

Using the three-step process we all learned in NCO Leadership Schools, Squadron Officer School, or the War College, I will now . . .

1. Tell you what I'm going to tell you.
2. Tell you.
3. Then, tell you what I told you.

First up: THE TELLING YOU WHAT I'M GOING TO TELL YOU PART

Overview

My purpose in writing this Field Manual is to provide you with a clear sense of the primary components of becoming a franchise owner. It's written primarily for novices to the franchise world; although, I think industry veterans already in this space might find some useful nuggets in here, too.

The six primary goals are to:

- Provide an insider's view into the magnitude of the franchise ecosystem.
- Offer a concise summary of the most pertinent terms, definitions, and general principles of franchising.
- Drill down into the most important details you must master in order to weigh the risks against the opportunities.
- Have this manual be a resource tailored to the needs of my fellow veterans considering owning a franchise.
- Help you: a) decide if franchising is for you, and if so, b) lay out the risks and differences between franchise opportunities.
- Expose you to employment opportunities in the franchise world.

I'm here to show you how to ask the right questions that get you meaningful answers.

This manual is not, by any means, all encompassing for every facet of the franchise world. Nor will you find me telling you what franchise to buy.

It is also not legal advice. My attorney insisted I add that caveat to keep me out of "franchise jail," as I call it. But it will give you a much deeper, insider understanding of how all the various machinations, expectations, prerogatives, and demands of franchising come together in such a way that makes franchising such an incredible economic engine.

Your Franchise Simulator Awaits

I not only flew in the Air Force and at Delta, but I was also a simulator instructor for both. I must confess: It was always a little sadistic fun to go off syllabus and load up a crew with unusual emergencies to see how they handled them. But, in my defense, some of those rides produced really great teachable moments.

This manual is going to feel a little like one of those "sim" rides with all sorts of "engine fires," "loss of hydraulics," and "bells and alarms" being thrown at you. This might get you to think franchising is too scary because of all the cautions I'm giving you. Instead, think of it like this: We send pilots through simulator training to expose them to all manner of problems, big and small, so they learn how to deal with them and safely land the airplane.

I'm doing that a little bit with you here. I'm merely warning you about things to look for along your flight path (franchise inquiry journey). When you experience the things I will be discussing in this manual, it won't feel foreign to you, and you should have the knowledge you need to navigate your way to a safe franchise landing.

Rules of Engagement

This manual is built to bring together the essentials you need to be able to assess if opting into a franchise business is the right decision for you and your family. It takes as its operating premise that, while you may be familiar with franchising through your interaction with various brands as a consumer, a clear sense of how things operate behind the logos is hard to come by.

Franchisors, franchisees, franchise attorneys, franchise consultants/brokers/advisers/coaches, franchise umbrella organizations, franchise sales organizations, franchise development companies, private equity firms, franchise PR firms, and franchise marketers all speak the language of franchising. Consider this your dual language dictionary for FSL (Franchising as a Second Language).

Here's what we will cover:

- CHAPTERS 1, 2 and 3 define the general concepts in franchising.
- CHAPTER 4 gives a surprising history of the impact of veterans on franchising.
- CHAPTER 5 addresses the myths surrounding the enterprise, some of which can lead to negative outcomes.
- CHAPTER 6 covers how to vet a franchise opportunity (pun intended).
- CHAPTER 7 illustrates how I would read a Franchise Disclosure Document (FDD), the document all franchisors must provide you before they can sell you a franchise.
- CHAPTERS 8 and 9 expose you to a broad list of franchise categories and offer tips on how to find the right franchise for you.
- CHAPTER 10 discusses financing for your franchise. On this topic let me say up front most franchise owners found the funding they needed to get started beyond their own resources. Franchising isn't just for the well-to-do (a common myth).
- CHAPTER 11 introduces you to the latest buzz within the franchise world, "Responsible Franchising."
- CHAPTER 12 explores other opportunities for veterans in the franchise industry beyond franchise ownership.
- CHAPTER 13 gives a shoutout to some of today's veterans making their mark on the industry.
- CHAPTER 14 is an interview with Jimmy Weeks, fellow Air Force Veteran and thought leader in the franchise industry.
- CHAPTER 15 provides a pro/con comparison of franchising versus DIY.
- CHAPTER 16 presents my parting thoughts.

At the end of the manual you'll find five appendices covering:

1. What It Takes To Be a Rock Star Franchisee
2. Questions To Ask Franchisors
3. Questions To Ask Franchisees
4. Questions To Ask Franchise Brokers
5. Glossary of Terms

This manual is a checklist of sorts regarding things you need to be aware of as you go about investigating your options. If this manual is to truly hit its target, it must also be a gut check and a reality check. It's meant to help you gain insight into your opportunities and to make sure you are ready to take this step, armed with solid information, clear in the mission, trusting in those you've chosen to work with.

Your Invitation To Engage

This Field Manual is for my fellow veterans to help them assess their opportunities to become business owners through franchising. This is your invitation to engage with the material you need to possess as you investigate the various franchise opportunities out there.

Keep in mind, I am not writing about you buying into national food brands, like McDonald's® or Dunkin'®, or big hotel brands, etc. Those brands operate at a very different business and capital funding level than I have intimate experience with. I am focusing on low cost to mid-range franchises, as that is what I know, especially in the service space. If you are looking for information about those big, international-type brands, you won't find much of it here, although I do think some of what I offer still applies.

It is my goal to share what I've learned so you have a leg up in this process.

Certain Terms Used Throughout the Book

Ripping language directly out of my old C-141 Dash One Operating Manual, the following are definitions to keep in mind while using this manual. I've altered them somewhat to apply them to the business of buying a franchise safely instead of the business of operating an aircraft safely.

Warnings, Cautions, and Notes

Warnings, Cautions, and Notes will always appear in the text where appropriate and will normally follow the items to which they apply.

The following definitions apply to "Warnings," "Cautions," and "Notes" found throughout the manual.

WARNING

Highlighting an area that, if overlooked, or if the question at hand is not fully resolved, might lead to a poor and costly business decision.

CAUTION

Highlighting an area that deserves closer examination to resolve open questions.

NOTE

A message that is considered essential to emphasize.

Now, on to the TELLING YOU part . . .

Chapter 1

What Is a Franchise?

The Federal Trade Commission defines a franchise as having three elements in a business relationship in which:

1. The franchisee is granted the rights to use the franchisor's trademark to offer goods or services under that trademark; and
2. The franchisor exerts a significant degree of control, or significant assistance in the operations of the franchised business; and
3. The franchisee makes a payment to the franchisor. [1]

The basic outline of the franchise business model was first established in the United States by none other than Benjamin Franklin, a fellow veteran.[2] He formed an agreement with a local printer to publish his works. The printer was responsible for managing the shop, had to purchase all the equipment from Franklin, and the printer could engage in no other business. That's the basic framework for today's franchise business model. Note: The part about engaging in no other business refers to no other *competing* business in today's practices.

Issac Singer of the Singer Sewing Machine Company is credited by many to be the first to really franchise to scale. While Singer was not a veteran, the Singer Sewing Machine Company did play an important role in WWII when it switched from making sewing machines to manufacturing parts for weapons and aircraft.[3]

Franchising really began to take hold when General Motors created the first dealerships at the turn of the 20th century[4] and was deployed into the food space by WWI veteran, Howard Johnson.[5] The acceleration in opportunities occurred post-World War II with the return of our soldiers, sailors, and airmen, and the expansion of goods, food, and services chains as the Baby Boom gets booming.

Today there are almost 4,000 active franchise concepts and sorting through them can be daunting. For those who are seeking to leverage established systems to gain an entrepreneurial foothold, franchises can be the gateway to financial independence.

The fees associated with buying a franchise are a trade-off: Some risk is mitigated by working within an established system, and big gains are expected with better brand recognition, proven systems, and other competitive advantages.

All businesses start from scratch. Franchises are designed to jump start the business by allowing franchisees to forego the establishing steps and concentrate on the running steps (unit growth and performance).

NOTE

A word about the phrase "proven systems." This term is one that gets thrown around much too easily, in my opinion. Virtually every franchise you investigate will make this claim. If they all have "proven" systems, then why do some franchise brands fail? "Proven" may just be in the eye of the beholder. What works in Miami might not work in Buffalo. What works in a local restaurant might not work at scale in other regions. Or, just maybe, it really isn't proven, and someone is just making shit up. For our purposes here, recognize that it's up to YOU to play Sherlock Holmes and determine if the franchise you're considering really has a proven system. And I'll show you some easy ways to do just that later on.

How Veterans Are Uniquely Positioned To Thrive in Franchising

Your time in the service, whether it was for 20 years, or a single tour, exposed you to near daily contact with concepts and approaches that are directly transferrable to franchising:

• Trust and reliance on established processes

• The ability to follow guidelines

• Trust in the chain of command

• Accountability for your role and your performance

• No one goes it alone: team dynamics determine outcomes

It is for these reasons, among others we'll get into in CHAPTER 4, that veterans are a target for franchisors, franchise brokers, and franchise sales organizations (FSOs). Your service, in many ways, has trained you to be able to execute the franchise model. Of course, not everyone's service is the same, and service alone is not a guarantor of success. It is, however, a marker for those attributes that make for successful franchise operators.

The FTC offers some valuable information for potential franchise buyers on their website. Give it a look. Visit ftc.gov/business-guidance/resources/consumers-guide-buying-franchise.

Next up, the world of franchising.

CHAPTER 2

THE WORLD OF FRANCHISING

There are three reasons you need to be well versed in the terms and definitions of franchising:

1. You need to be able to understand the language, so you aren't entirely reliant on experts. This is your risk. Own the responsibility to be an active participant.
2. Gaining clarity early in your process will help avoid pitfalls and will debunk some of the myths.
3. Provides a sense of the scope and scale of the industry, its best practices, and opportunities.

In this chapter I'll share with you a bird's eye view of the scope and scale of franchising and provide a rundown of the various participants in the industry, their roles, and how you can leverage their expertise.

Let's throttle up!

Did I just detect an eye roll?

Gotcha!

Scope and Scale

Franchising in the United States accounts for over $850 billion in economic output and employs over 8.4 million people.[1] Franchising is the single most powerful economic engine ever imagined. It derives its strength from the development and deployment, through scale, of reliable business systems.

To enter this industry you should be cognizant of how pervasive franchising is and the undeniable opportunity it holds for establishing a means of generating wealth.

Veterans own over 66,000 franchises producing more than $41 billion in GDP.[2] According to VetFran (discussed later in this chapter), veterans account for approximately 14% of franchise ownership while only representing 7% of the general population.[3] That means veterans are twice as likely as non-veterans to own a franchise. Vets and franchising do quite well together.

Participants

Franchising is a unique world unto itself. To navigate the franchise exploration process you need to know the participants involved. Everyone mentioned below is making money by being involved. That is not a bad thing. How these people act and where their incentives lie are of more use to you than simply writing it all off as a hustle. The industry is loaded with good and honest people doing things the right way.

There are, however, some who place the dollar above all else.

I'll offer some tips on how to identify the latter throughout this book.

Franchisors

What, exactly, do franchisors do? They recruit others (franchisees) to join forces in growing their brand and assist those franchisees in building their own franchised businesses.

Franchisors do this by licensing their franchisees the rights to use their trademark(s) and trade secrets, sharing systems, vendors, marketing systems, and buyers' groups, etc., and training and supporting their franchisees on how to run their business.

Broadly, there are two types of franchisors: Single brands, often with their founders still in place (or the corporate line of succession), and franchise umbrella brands managing multiple brands.

We are driven by compelling stories, our own and others'. There are scores of franchise founders who have overcome adversity or who've been in the right place at the right time to seize an opportunity others missed. It runs the gamut. Remember, you are buying into a system and process, and that system had to have first been built by someone.

The most successful veteran franchisor I know is Gordon Logan. Gordon launched Sport Clips® in 1993 and it now boasts over 1,900 locations nationwide. *1,900!*

Gordon matched men's and boys' needs to go to the barber with the generally assumed enjoyment of sports and, voilà, a franchise legend was born. Gordon was an Air Force C-130 driver.

Gordon is such a great example of that single brand founder who succeeded in a very big way. But remember, the real focus of this book is on what it takes to find and join an existing franchise organization that fits your needs, just like the franchise owners of all those 1,900 Sport Clips locations, many of whom are veterans.

*That's Gordon and me at the 2024 Pebble Beach Concours
d'Elegance where he was showing his beautiful 1940 Packard
1806 Custom Super Eight Darrin Convertible*

A growing trend in the franchise space is the use of franchise umbrella (or portfolio) organizations. Often with Private Equity (PE) involved, these groups sometimes manage their portfolio as separate entities or, more commonly, combine and scale resources to create powerhouse franchise teams and brands.

Neighborly® Brands is the largest home services franchise umbrella brand in the world. It includes names like The Grounds Guys® (I use them for my three-acre yard, the crew is run by a veteran injured in Iraq, and they're great!), Mosquito Joe, Glass Doctor®, Dryer Vent Wizard®, Mr. Electric®, Mr. Handyman®, and many more.

With 19 brands and roughly 5,500 franchise units in six countries, Neighborly just surpassed $4 billion in combined sales for 2023 and boasts having over 400 veteran franchisees within their brands.[4] Neighborly was formerly the Dwyer Group, founded by Don Dwyer (you guessed it, a veteran). More on Don a little later in my VetFran discussion.

By the way, can you tell I admire Neighborly?

Other names in the franchise umbrella and portfolio space include Buzz Franchise Brands (four varied services), Driven Brands (automotive), Empower Brands (home and commercial services), Eversmith Brands (mix of residential and commercial services), Evive Brands (health and home services), Extraordinary Brands (health and wellness), FirstService Brands (property services), Five Star Franchising (a mix of six brands), Franworth (services, food, and health), GoTo Foods (formerly Focus Brands), Horsepower Brands (home services), Moran Family of Brands, Premium Service Brands (home services), Phoenix Franchise Brands (a mix of services), Propelled Brands (four diverse offerings), ResiBrands (home services), Self Esteem Brands (fitness, health, and wellness), Unleashed Brands (youth enrichment), and, of course, Veteran Service Brands (mostly commercial with some residential services).

Franchising is very big business built out of countless small businesses.

Private Equity

Now might be a good time to discuss Private Equity (PE). According to Alicia Miller, best-selling author of *Big Money in Franchising*, it wasn't long ago that PE shied away from investing in franchise models, but no more.[5] When PE looks at franchises they are generally looking for concepts that:

- are straightforward, easy to replicate,
- are sustainable in the market,
- have a track record of success (a critical mass of units),
- have white space (room for continued growth), and
- have successful franchisees (happy and making money).

Alicia was gracious enough to offer the following specifically for this manual and your consideration:

If PE is invested in the concept, this signals PE sees growth potential. However, don't take the shortcut of choosing that franchise just because it has a PE sponsor! You need to do your own homework and determine whether it's a fit for your own objectives. Also, remember that PE's profit-seeking agenda has a real impact on franchisees. In theory, PE will invest in accel-erators which can benefit franchisees. But sometimes PE's agenda conflicts with franchisee interests. Even when PE-backed management teams make changes that are intended to be positive for the system, franchisees may still find changes stressful. Take the time to interview franchisees who were involved in the brand both before and after PE acquisition to understand what has changed and whether franchisees believe they are getting a good return on their investment of time, effort, and money.

This further drives home the point: You must know all the parties invested in your franchise.

Franchisees

The promise of franchising is to become a business owner but not be entirely on your own. People are drawn to this promise from all walks of life and for as many reasons as there are people.

It is personal.

It should be.

There are some consistent patterns in who self-selects to become a franchisee:

- They want to be their own boss, but they don't wish to go it alone.
- They view business ownership as a path to wealth.
- They yearn for a change in their lifestyle.
- They wish to minimize start-up risks.
- They no longer wish to work for someone else.
- They seek a new purpose in life.

You can want all of the above but, unless you opt in to a model that can show you how it works, that it has worked, and the leadership involved is engaged on a daily basis to keep it working, all your wants, desires, yearnings, dreams, and wishes for success won't matter. Who you choose to go into business with is mission critical.

Area Representatives

Some franchise systems offer you the opportunity to be an Area Representative. Depending upon the particular brand, you may not need to be a franchisee to hold this position.

Essentially, you act as the sub-franchisor in your area. You buy the rights to develop your area and are in the business of recruiting new franchisees and assisting the franchisor with supporting these locations. Details vary by brand, but Area Representatives usually collect a portion of the franchise fee and typically enjoy some split with the franchisor of the royalties. Most Area Development Agreements will require some degree of minimum performance to develop more locations.

Multi-Unit Operators

When you hear the expression "multi-unit operator" or "multi-unit franchisee," they typically aren't talking about someone with two or three locations. It's more along the lines of five, 10, 15, or more units. Some multi-unit owners are individuals and others are very large investment groups. The investment groups are some of the heaviest of hitters in the franchise world. Franchising.com puts out its annual Mega 99 Rankings for the industry each year. At the top is the Flynn Group with over 2,600 big name locations. At the other end, there was a four-way tie for Number 99. Each had 132 units for 2023.[6]

There are also plenty of very wealthy multi-unit franchisees who own fewer than 20 units. You can absolutely become a multi-unit operator if you find the right franchise(s) and you scale wisely.

Ask about multi-unit opportunities. These are very common in the food and wellness/health spaces.

Franchise Professionals

On your entrepreneurial journey you are going to encounter a number of people engaged in different professions, all supporting the ultimate sale of franchises. There are also trade associations that support franchise owners. It is a culture and society built around entrepreneurial effort and the effort to sustain both franchisors and franchisees. Knowing the players will help you determine the weight you give to each of their offerings.

Franchise Brokers/Consultants/Coaches/Advisors

Within the vast world of franchise sales you may encounter folks who describe themselves as Franchise Brokers, Franchise Consultants, Franchise Coaches, and/or Franchise Advisors. There's even a Franchise Whisperer in Australia. You might think of them as you would military recruiters.

Technically, the Franchise Broker/Consultant/Advisor/Coach doesn't sell you the franchise. The franchisor is the one legally selling it to you. The broker types are the facilitators.

The FTC does not recognize the claimed differences between brokers, coaches, consultants, or advisors. Title 16 of C.F.R. § Section 436.2(j) states: *The term franchise broker means any person other than a franchisor or franchisee who sells, offers for sale, or arranges the sale of a franchise.*

In light of this official definition, I'm going to differentiate anyone in these categories simply as a franchise "broker." I may also use the term "company representative" to identify in-house brokers from outside brokers.

Brokers will help you find a franchise and collect a fee from the franchisor as some percentage of the franchise fee that you spend (typically 30% to 60%, but it can vary to as high as 100%). There might also be some out there who charge you a fee up front so you don't waste their time.

Should you work with brokers or go it alone is one of the first essential questions to ask yourself. With almost 4,000 active franchise brands out there, trying to do this on your own might quickly become overwhelming. I'm going to go against my own self-interests here and recommend you find a broker you can work with and trust.

For the first six years of my current franchisor journey, we did not list any of our franchises with any Franchise Broker Network (FBN). Our franchise fees were too low to attract any broker interest. That means tens of thousands of prospects have never heard of us.

We sell via our own advertising, partnerships, social media, and word of mouth. We also sell from one brand to another inside VSB to existing owners. Only very recently have we started to dip our toes into the FBN space with one of our brands.

I know many very good brokers; some are veterans themselves. Try a search for "veteran franchise broker," or peruse LinkedIn® to help you find a broker you can work with.

I wish to steer clear of specific recommendations in this manual so as to not accidentally exclude good people or inadvertently steer you to a less than ideal broker. There are some awesome non-veteran brokers out there as well, of course.

If you are already working with someone in this field, there's a pretty good chance your initial internet searches led you to them by way of a Lead Referral Network (LRN). LRNs invest heavily in online marketing by buying up search terms like "franchises for sale," "best franchises," "franchises for veterans," etc., and using targeted ads on search engines and social media to find veterans like you interested in business ownership.

NOTE

Unless and until you sign a contract with a broker, you are under no obligation to work with them.

Getting back to my initial question of whether to use the broker or go it alone, I recommend *both*. Work with your broker, do some serious digging on your own to validate what you're hearing, and do some comparisons.

Brokers are sometimes compared with real estate agents. I tend to think brokers have to work considerably harder. The franchise industry rule of thumb is one deal closes for every 100 leads. That means multiple attempts are made by the broker to even contact each party who made some sort of inquiry. Multiply that times 100 and you get the picture. That, along with dealing with the unserious (aka "wantrepreneurs"), the unfundable, and the undecideds (stuck in analysis paralysis), makes the business of helping someone find a business that much more challenging.

A real estate agent just needs someone who desires a house, can get a loan, put in a solid bid, and fog a mirror. There's no profiling or vetting allowed. You need not pass a personality test to buy a home, nor worry the seller won't sell because they don't think you share the same core values.

The franchise broker has to play amateur psychologist to understand what makes you tick, research what funding you qualify for, walk you through multiple concepts, and get you through the vetting process with the franchisor.

That's a LOT of work and their "big fee" doesn't seem so big when you look at the challenges in closing a deal.

There are some big names in the broker networks. I'll start with the "Frans." You've got FranChoice, FranNet, FranServe, and NextFran. Then, alphabetically, we have Business Alliance Inc. (BAI), Franchise

Brokers Association (FBA), International Franchise Professionals Group (IFPG), The Entrepreneur's Source (TES), The Franchise Consulting Company (FCC), and Transworld Business Advisors. There are likely others out there I may have overlooked.

These organizations sign up franchise brands to join their network. Franchisors typically pay fees just to be listed in their directory. Franchisors often list on multiple networks. Not uncommon to see 200 to 800 franchise brands in a network.

Recall, I mentioned almost 4,000 franchise brands are active? It's impossible to dig deep into all those brands so, in theory and application (hopefully), the FBN has a great portfolio from which you can choose to explore. If you can't find anything you like in their network, there's good news. You've likely only been exposed to fewer than 5% to 15% of the possibilities.

Some FBNs do allow their brokers to present opportunities outside their portfolio. Others do not. Ask yours if they are limited. Not a deal breaker, per se, if they're not allowed to venture out, but it's knowledge you should gather, nevertheless.

There are also lots of independent brokers, too, with no particular franchise network affiliation.

My Likes and Dislikes About the Franchise Broker Networks

First, the likes.

They are free to you.

Kinda.

Sort of.

The franchisor pays them from the franchise fee you pay the franchisor so, ultimately, it's really your money paying them.

Brokers live and breathe franchising and attend conventions and conferences. They know what brands are "hot" in their portfolio (which may or not be a good thing—more on that later). They understand Franchise Disclosure Documents (FDDs are covered in detail in CHAPTER 6). Many attend professional training courses through the International Franchise Association® (IFA) to gain the designation of CFE (Certified Franchise Executive™). Brokers help you whittle down your search and open your eyes to franchise concepts you might not have heard of or passed on without knowing the story behind the brand. I interact with many brokers both socially and professionally and admire their hard work and dedication to their clients.

Now, my dislikes.

The broker system drives up the costs of doing business. That means those costs are passed along to you, the franchise buyer. Plain and simple.

This, despite the fact there's an imbalance in the marketplace. Supply greatly outweighs demand. There are far more franchise opportunities out there than there are buyers. Most franchise brands don't hit their sales goals. Some have zero sales. The notion of the elasticity of demand driving down prices (as it should) takes the opposite direction in great part due to the broker networks, in my humble opinion. That's just the world we live in. Franchise brokering is hard work, and no one is going to do it on the cheap precisely because buyers are hard to find and getting them across the finish line is never guaranteed.

Now, layer in the fact when one works on commission, it makes sense to go after bigger commissions. It's human nature. There exists a financial incentive to steer franchise prospects towards the higher commissions. Does that conflict with your goals? Maybe. Depends on the broker.

Don't be afraid to ask what the commission is for each brand being presented to you. Remember, *it's your money*. The true professionals won't be bothered by this and will embrace transparency. I've made my point here. Do with it what you wish.

A second possible concern is when brokers are restricted from presenting offerings outside their defined network, as I mentioned earlier. Some networks are very restrictive. Others aren't. I imagine the counter-argument goes something like this: If you can't find a franchise you like within the 200 to 800 we have, what makes you think you'll find one outside that circle?

Again, knowledge is power.

One final observation: Brokers and Franchise Sales Organizations (FSOs are discussed next) are often enlisted to help emerging franchise brands grow and grow fast. That can lead to a brand getting out over its skis. Grow too fast and the back-end support can lag. Systems that worked for 30 locations have to be retooled for 200 locations. Often these brands that have a fast-growth mindset will push multi-unit sales. It's important you are clear on how you want the process of finding a franchise to go when dealing with your broker.

A Word About "Multi-Pack" Deals

Many brands will encourage you to secure multiple territories to develop later (depending upon the industry). They may want to sell you a "three-pack," a "five-pack," or a "ten-pack" Nothing magical about those particular numbers, it's just what I see happening.

Be very careful here. Your enthusiasm to join the brand can lure you into biting off more than you can chew.

Unless you are well capitalized and can risk losing all or most of your investment in a multi-pack deal, I'd tread lightly and get a single unit up and running before rushing into additional obligations.

Franchise Sales Organizations (FSOs)

Sometimes called franchise development companies, FSOs are hired by the franchisor to sell units and develop support services matched to that growth. They differ somewhat from brokers, as they are an outsourced package the franchisor delegates all, or most, of the sales, training, and support to, and have their own brokers working within the

FSO. Of course there are always exceptions to this and there are any number variations of this formula.

FSOs focus on the franchising side of the business, creating the FDD along with legal counsel, creating or fine-tuning the operating manual, establishing processes, and developing growth strategies through marketing locally and for franchise sales. They allow the franchisor to stick to their core competencies and expertise and outsource the franchise piece.

That comes with a price tag. FSOs aren't cheap for the franchisor. Good FSOs can help catapult the brand's growth. FSOs will usually extract some or most of the franchise fee, they take a cut of the royalty stream, and may also have ownership in the brand. If a franchisor has a great concept but is stuck at 10 units and can't break free, FSOs might be the answer.

At one level, it's a math problem for the franchisor. Is 100% of the franchise fees and royalties for 10 units worth more or less than 20% of the franchise fees and 60% of the royalties for 100 units?

Big names in the FSO space include BrandOne, Franchise Performance Group, FranDevCo, FranGrowth, MSA Worldwide (they were kind enough to let me use their glossary of franchise terms for Appendix 5), Pinnacle, Rhino7, REP'M, United Franchise Group, and others.

Not to confuse things, but most FSOs also use the broker networks. You might not even know the FSO is in the background. If they do have ownership in the brand you're interested in, that will be disclosed in the FDD.

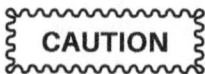

CAUTION

There exists a murky cottage industry of FSOs that don't deserve to be named here. They recruit naïve entrepreneurs into hiring them to franchise their business. These entrepreneurs get caught up in franchise fever and will hand over upwards of $100,000 or more to get their FDD and ops manual created. They'll get a listing on some random franchise website and then reality sets in. They now need additional, significant sums to market their brand. And from what I see, many of these brands are going nowhere no matter how much they spend. Some of the 450 new franchise concepts launched in 2024 come from this segment. This is my caution for folks interested in buying a franchise as well as entrepreneurs who get swept up into "fran fever" before being truly prepared to franchise. *Just because you can franchise, doesn't mean you should.* Sage advice from my franchise attorney, Charles Internicola.

Direct Franchise Corporate Sales

Many franchise brands handle sales directly with their own in-house brokers, including mine. Many larger brands have abandoned the broker network altogether. Some left because they want to control all the sales steps. Other reasons might be based upon inertia. They've got more people wanting to join than they can process, so they don't need additional leads. Some brands are like that.

Direct sales are the means for franchisors to control two main factors:

- costs associated with brokers, and
- the vetting of potential franchise partners themselves.

With sales remaining in-house, franchisors have a direct sense of who they are dealing with, *sans* middleman, from day one.

Franchise Attorneys

Buying a franchise places you in a binding contract with the franchisor. Each party has responsibilities and obligations to the other. A franchise attorney, one who specializes in the language of franchises, is often an integral part of the last two steps when buying a franchise: reviewing the FDD and signing the franchise agreement.

You may use any attorney you wish or none at all. Franchising is a very specific niche in the legal world and, as with so much else, using a seasoned expert can help clear your path. I highly recommend you get an attorney who specializes in franchise law. I sometimes see franchise prospects working with general practice or contract attorneys who don't fully understand the unique language and nuances of franchise law. Your cousin Morty, the real estate attorney, is not going to fully understand what the FDD is telling him. When choosing a franchise attorney, get answers to these questions:

- What is their experience with franchising?
- Do they represent just franchisees? Any franchisors? Both? (It's OK if they represent both—I just like to know who I'm hiring and their background.)
- How often do they review FDDs?
- Do they have any pertinent experience with the industry you're exploring?

They need not score 100% on all of the above. Just find one you feel you can trust more than anything.

The International Franchise Association (IFA)

The IFA's Mission Statement is to *protect, enhance, and promote franchising.*

The IFA supports both franchisees and franchisors.

I highly suggest you head over to IFA's website, franchise.org, and spend some time there. Lots of great information to be had.

VetFran

The one organization I wish to spend more time on is VetFran. Born out of the IFA and the brainchild of Don Dwyer, Sr., founder of the Dwyer Group, now Neighborly (mentioned earlier) and DreamMaker® Bath and Kitchen (now run by Don's son, Doug Dwyer, and his wife, Gayla),VetFran has a very specific mission: to educate veterans and franchisors regarding the crossover of skills developed from military service that transfer to successful franchise ownership. VetFran has been around since 1991 and serves both veterans and franchisors.

As an Army veteran himself, Don was one of the first franchise pioneers to understand the possibilities of leveraging veterans' military experiences for the collective benefit of both the veteran franchisee and the franchisor.

For veterans transitioning out of the service, franchise ownership can be a means to gaining a viable economic foothold in civilian life. VetFran encourages franchisors to offer discounts to veterans to help make ownership more affordable (we'll talk more about discounts in CHAPTER 10), and they work to educate veterans about the franchising world.

Franchisors join VetFran for a host of reasons (patriotism, corporate social responsibility, etc.), but another reason they might join is simply to have access to a unique pool of prospects with previous leadership experience, systems and process exposure, accountability, and teamwork skills. VetFran can be a valuable resource for veterans considering franchising as a way to own a small business and generate wealth.

Visit VetFran.org for more info.

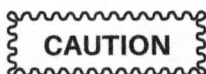

CAUTION

A listing on VetFran should not be construed as an endorsement, nor as an indicator that these franchises require less vetting on your part.

In the next chapter, we'll look at the various franchise models.

CHAPTER 3

FRANCHISE MODELS

The IFA identifies two types of franchise business models: the Business Format (the most common in terms of numbers and what one generally thinks of when they hear the word "franchise"), and the Product Distribution Format (larger in total dollar output than the Business Format Models but much smaller in unit numbers—think Coca-Cola®, Shell®, GM®, etc.).

I've expanded that list for our purposes here. These are the five types of franchise opportunities as I see them:

1. The Job Franchise
2. The Investment Franchise
3. Franchise Models
4. The Product Distribution Franchise
5. The Business Format Franchise
6. The Conversion Franchise

Each one of these model types fulfills a unique function in franchising. Each one addresses one segment on the business continuum—from owner-operators to sprawling corporate entities managing a portfolio of franchises—and everything in between. Some have varying degrees of overlap.

The Job Franchise

This is the owner-operator version of buying a franchise. Affectionately known as "Chuck in a Truck" (sometimes derisively), you are basically buying yourself a job.

Don't let that sound like a bad thing. The franchise gives the owner-operator help with branding, marketing, customer relationship management (CRM), and other systems that are typically way beyond the skill sets and financial resources needed to create these from the ground up as a solo entrepreneur. There are plenty of Chucks out there making big bucks.

There's nothing wrong with working in your business with a big dash of assistance if you love doing X yourself.

Branding, credibility, and training could be the main drivers for the owner-operator to choose this path.

Big advantages to this model are low start-up costs, no payroll to start, and generally very low overhead (often home-based). You are initially responsible for delivering the goods and/or services associated with the opportunity. Think select home and business services (dryer vent cleaning, furniture repair, window blinds, pressure washing, etc.)

Many (most?) owner-operator models are designed to transition to owner-manager as the business grows. Now, Chuck manages a number of trucks.

For those who dismiss the Job Franchise as something less worthy: What "job" allows you to set your own hours, set your own pay, choose your customers, and take vacations when you want—and makes you bulletproof from layoffs?

The owner-operator model has been my initial path for my businesses and the one I see aligning well for many of my fellow veterans.

The Investment Franchise

These are large-scale operations with substantial capital investment. You're certainly not hands-on operationally, and the business has its own corporate team to manage it. Well-capitalized individuals and corporate investors, likely with an established position in the market or similar operating structures, are the players in this sandbox. Some examples would be hotel chains or very big name restaurant chains.

The Distribution Franchise

Car dealerships, electronics, fuel, beverages, and appliance retailers fall under this category. These require a significant investment and a team to manage. This franchise type is not within the scope of this book.

The Business Format Franchise

This model is the one most people think of when they hear "franchise": All the goods, equipment, training, and back-office systems are provided by the franchisor, and the franchisee must utilize the entirety of those services. Fast food, coffee shops, business services, home services, and personal care are all represented in this model. This one can have a good deal of overlap with the Job Franchise Model as well as the Investment Franchise Model.

The Conversion Franchise

If you can't beat 'em, join 'em.

This model is for those who own an independent business but convert it to join a franchise within their industry. Maybe they tried going it alone and couldn't compete. They go through rebranding to switch to the new brand. The goal is to take advantage of the franchisor's brand, network, reach, systems, and support. This happens often in real estate, lawn care, dry cleaning, and healthcare settings.

The co-founders of Century 21®, Art Bartlett and Marsh Fisher (a WWII veteran), are credited with creating the concept of "conversion franchising." They consolidated independent real estate agencies under the Century 21 name. Mr. Bartlett is quoted in the *Los Angeles Times* in 1982 as saying, "Franchising has been the savior of free enterprise in this country. It has given the small businessman a way to survive."[1]

There is a lot of consolidation in the service space, placing more and more pressure on the local independent entrepreneur. This model often overlaps with the Job Franchise (with an eye to scale) and the Business Format Franchise.

Franchise Model Conclusion

Broadly, those are the types of models available as franchise opportunities.

Given this manual is focused on lower cost and mid-tier opportunities, not the massive capital investments associated with some models, it is important for you to make sure you know what slice of this pie you want to take on; what matches your skills, intentions, and capacity to operate.

Next, let's talk about some fascinating franchise history involving veterans and why the industry wants you on Team Franchise.

CHAPTER 4

VETERANS IN FRANCHISING

It is no understatement to say veterans made franchising what it is today.

Of the following big name, old school, iconic franchise brands, care to guess how many were founded by veterans: Avis®, Hilton Hotels®, Howard Johnson's®, ServiceMaster®, Friendly's® Ice Cream, Krispy Kreme®, Dairy Queen®, Carl's Jr.®, Baskin-Robbins®, Chick-fil-A®, Stanley Steemer®, Jack in the Box®, Holiday Inn®, KFC®, Sonic® Drive-In®, Burger King®, H&R Block®, McDonald's®, Enterprise® Car Rental, Hyatt Hotels®, IHOP®, Domino's®, Hardee's®, Circle K®, Taco Bell®, Arby's®, Wendy's®, and RE/MAX®?

If you said "all of them," you'd be correct.

But wait, there's more where that came from!

I'd like to now share with you what took me about one year of on-again, off-again research trying to determine which brands were founded or substantially impacted by veterans.

If you decide that franchising is the right decision for you and your family, I want you to know there is a depth here of veterans not only building iconic businesses but shaping and refining the idea of franchising itself. You'll be standing on the shoulders of giants.

I'll now share with you a brief overview of those veterans who've come before you and laid the groundwork for the franchise opportunities we have today.

The Early Years for Veterans in Franchising

Dale Carnegie, author of *How to Win Friends and Influence People,* launched his training career in 1912. He began licensing his training course to others in 1930 (a sort of proto-franchise arrangement; they began formally franchising in 2000). Carnegie is still influencing people over 100 years later with approximately 200 Dale Carnegie and Associates® franchise locations. Carnegie served in the Army during WWI (despite filing as a conscientious objector with a missing finger).[1]

Conrad Hilton was the force behind Hilton® Hotels. Conrad served in the Army during WWI as well. Founded in 1919, Hilton now lists 7,500 properties worldwide.[2]

Radio Shack® (now RadioShack®) first launched in 1921. Struggling with only nine stores in 1962, the Tandy Corporation bought Radio-Shack and changed the business model to focus on franchised retail stores. At its peak in 1999, RadioShack had roughly 8,000 stores. Charles Tandy, founder of the Tandy Corporation, was an officer in the Navy from 1941 to 1947.[3]

Howard Johnson, founder of his namesake restaurants, served in the American Expeditionary Force during WWI. Howard Johnson® (now HoJo®) was first launched in 1925 and has 280 locations.[4]

Howard Johnson's

The earliest service-based franchise I could identify was ServiceMaster. It was founded in 1929 by Marion Wade, a minor-league baseball player who enlisted in the Marines after his brother died in WWI. The war ended shortly after he finished boot camp at Parris Island. Service-Master lists over 7,000 locations nationwide.[5]

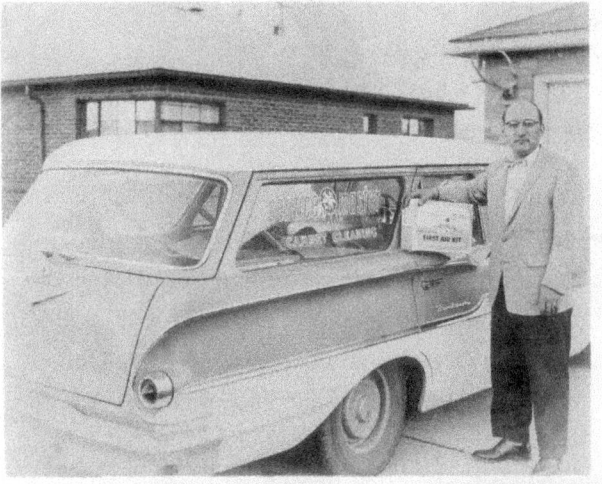

Marion Wade of ServiceMaster

Tom Carvel began selling ice cream from his vending truck in 1929. Over Memorial Day weekend in 1934, his truck broke down and he was forced to sell the melting ice cream on the spot. He quickly discovered people liked softer ice cream. WWII begins and Carvel finds himself working with refrigeration and concessions in the Army. This helped advance his knowledge for his soft ice cream venture. In 1947, Carvel® became the first to franchise ice cream from a retail shop. They list 345 locations on their website.[6]

Tom Carvel

Irl H. Marshall, WWI Navy veteran, founded the Home Services Company, a carpet cleaning service, in 1930. In the mid-1940s, Marshall changed the name to Duraclean® International and expanded to other cleaning services beyond carpets and rugs. Duraclean now has almost 300 franchise locations.[7] Marshall once served as the Chairman of the IFA.

Steak 'n Shake® was started in 1934 by Gus Belt, a four-year veteran of the Marines. Steak 'n Shake now has 370 locations; approximately 50 are franchised and the rest are company-owned.[8]

Friendly's® Ice Cream, a New England favorite, first got its start as Friendly Ice Cream in 1935 at the height of the Great Depression. Brothers Curtis and S. Prestley Blake were the founders. Curtis served four years in the Army Air Forces during WWII. Friendly changed to "Friendly's" in 1989 to match how the locals were pronouncing it. Boasting 850 locations at its peak, Friendly's is now down to about 100 locations after losing approximately 300 in just the last decade.[9]

Krispy Kreme traces its roots as far back as 1937, also in the middle of the Great Depression. Vernon Rudolph began selling Krispy Kreme franchises in 1940 and later went off to war to serve in the Army Air Forces. Krispy Kreme has over 14,000 outlets in 39 countries.[10]

1938 brings us the Culligan Man®. Emmett Culligan served in WWI and discovered the benefits of soft water from his experience with his wife giving birth at a hospital a few years prior. He launched the Culligan® Zeolite Company (zeolite being the secret to soft water). The company changed its name to Culligan® Incorporated and later to the Culligan® International Company. As one of the largest suppliers of silica gel, the company was awarded an Army-Navy certificate for its contribution to the war effort. They report roughly 800 locations in 90 countries.[11]

Dairy Queen opened in 1940, then paused during WWII so that its co-founder, Sherwood "Sherb" Noble, could serve his country during WWII. After the war, Sherb got back to scooping "soft-serve" for his customers. Dairy Queen was the leading fast-food franchise in the early 1960s.[12] Warren Buffet's Berkshire Hathaway bought DQ® in 1997. Buffet served in the Nebraska and New York National Guard from 1951 to 1956. There are 5,700 DQ locations in the United States.

1941 saw the first Dickey's Barbecue Pit® in Dallas, opened by Travis Dickey, a WWI veteran. Dickey's didn't begin franchising until 53 years later, in 1994. Travis' grandson, Roland Dickey Jr., is still active in this family-run operation boasting almost 900 locations in 44 states.[13]

Up Next: The Greatest Generation of Veteran Franchisors

Post-World War II saw an explosion of ingenuity and entrepreneurship using the franchise model. Imagine how many times this question was posed between 1941 and 1945: *So, what are you going to do after the war?*

Apparently, a lot of veterans had very big dreams.

With only an eighth grade education, Carl Karcher borrowed $311 to start a hot dog stand in 1941. He added a few more dog stands, then closed them to open Carl's Drive-In Barbecue. After his Army tour in WWII, he returned to open a smaller version of the BBQ concept in 1945 and named it Carl's Jr. This brand now stands at over 1,100 restaurants.[14] Carl's Jr. will go on to be the longest surviving franchise brand ever conceived and will last at least through the year 2505. Ten point bonus if you know this movie reference without an internet search! Some people say this movie has turned out to be a prophetic documentary. Not me, of course. Just some people.

1943 brings us the launch of Pizzeria Uno®, founded by Ike Sewell and Ric Riccardo, now known simply as Uno's®. They didn't begin franchising until 1980. Sourcing was hard for the veteran connection. The Wikipedia page (not my favorite reference) for Uno's only mentions Riccardo as Sewell's friend and former "WWII G.I." The Uno website claims over 130 restaurants.

First launched in 1945, Baskin-Robbins® gets its name from its founders, Burt Baskin, a Lieutenant Commander in the Naval Reserve, and Irv Robbins, a Sergeant in the Army. Both served in WWII. There are almost 2,800 Baskin-Robbins locations in the United States.[15]

S. Truett Cathy, an Army WWII veteran, founded Chick-fil-A® in 1946.[16] Chick-fil-A has roughly 3,000 locations and is the envy of the franchise world for its unit level economics.

S. Truett Cathy

Warren Avis, an officer and bombardier in the Army Air Forces during WWII, founded Avis Airlines Rent a Car, the first to rent cars at an airport. Avis® now has about 5,500 locations in 165 countries and is part of the Avis Budget Group®.[17] (See also Budget below)

Stanley Steemer® was founded in 1947 by Jack Bates, who served as a Navy Ensign during WWII. They have approximately 275 locations nationwide.[18]

Harmon Dobson, WWII veteran (no branch given), founded Whataburger® in 1950. It offered something people had never seen: a burger that was so big, they had to hold its five-inch bun with two hands. Whataburger has over 1,000 locations in 15 states.[19]

Robert O. Peterson founded Jack in the Box® in 1951. Peterson was a Naval Intelligence Officer in WWII. Jack in the Box lists over 2,100 locations, with the vast majority in California.[20]

Founded in 1951, Circle K has 7,000 locations and was started by Fred Hervey, who served in the Navy during WWII.[21]

1952 proved to be a very big year for future franchise brands.

At the age of 69, George W. Church Sr. opened the first Church's® Fried Chicken To-Go in San Antonio across the street from the Alamo.

George Church Jr. served as a Navy mechanic from 1951 to 1955 and took over the business when his dad died unexpectedly in 1956 and led the company to franchising. Church's now has more than 1,500 locations in 23 countries.[22]

The co-founder of Holiday Inn®, Charles Kemmons Wilson, served during WWII. His partner, Wallace E. Wilson, always referred to himself as "a poor little peckerwood boy from Mississippi."[23] Not sure what that has to do with veterans, but I love that humble, self-deprecating attitude from a wildly successful executive. Between Holiday Inn and Holiday Inn Express®, there are now approximately 4,300 locations around the world after springing from the very first Holiday Inn in Memphis in 1952.[24]

While Colonel Sanders wasn't really a Colonel in the Army, he did enlist by lying about his age (16), served in Cuba, and was discharged as a Private.[25] Kentucky Fried Chicken® first opened in 1952, when Sanders was 65 years old. KFC is found in 25,000 locations around the world.[26] Sanders was famously rejected 1,009 times trying to sell his recipe.[27]

The founder of Sonic Drive-In, Troy Smith, enlisted in the Army during WWII. First opened in 1953, Sonic now has over 3,500 locations.[28]

Both co-founders of Burger King were WWII vets. James McLamore served in the Navy. Dave Edgarton served in the Army. You will find roughly 20,000 BKs around the world. They first opened in 1954.[29]

1954 also brought us the very first pizza franchise. Shakey's® Pizza Parlor was founded by Sherwood "Shakey" Johnson and his partner, Ed Plummer. The nickname Shakey was given to Johnson because he had the "shakes" after a bout of malaria he suffered during WWII while serving in the Navy aboard the USS *Alnitah*.[30] Shakey met his future wife at the American Legion. Shakey's has roughly 60 locations.[31] Fun fact: The lead singer for the band Journey, Arnel

Campaner Piñada, got his start singing at a Shakey's in the Philippines in 1982 and joined the band in 2007.[32] Don't stop believing.

Brothers Henry and Richard Bloch, founders of H&R Block® (1955), were both veterans. Henry flew 32 combat missions as a navigator on the B-17 Flying Fortress (an amazing feat few ever matched), and Richard was a First Lieutenant in the Army during the Korean War.[33] H&R Block has over 8,700 locations in the U.S.[34] Speaking of B-17s, don't miss the chance to visit the 390th Bomb Group display at the Pima Air Museum in Tucson. Humbling.

That same year, 1955, Ray Kroc opened his first McDonald's restaurant after first serving as the franchise agent for the McDonald brothers.[35] Brothers Richard and Maurice McDonald had opened their first restaurant in 1940, just prior to WWII. Kroc eventually bought out the brothers in 1961 and set the course for making McDonald's (and the franchise industry at large) what it is today. Kroc lied about his age (15) to join the Red Cross ambulance service in WWI.[36] There are now 36,000 McDonald's around the world.[37] The McDonald brothers were not veterans, and Kroc was not the original founder, but his oversized influence on the franchise world warrants his inclusion in this list.

Old School McDonald's

Charles Loudermilk, WWII Navy veteran, launched Aaron Rents in 1955. He chose the name Aaron so it would show up first in the Yellow Pages®. For those veterans who don't know what the Yellow Pages are, ask your grandparents. Now called Aaron's Rent To Own®, they have approximately 1,210 company-owned and franchised stores in the U.S. and Canada.[38]

Waffle House® debuted in 1955, too. It was founded by two veterans: Joe Rogers, Sr., who served in the Army Air Forces in WWII, and Tom Forkner, who also served during the war in Army Intelligence (including the Manhattan Project). Waffle House now has over 2,000 locations in 25 states.[39]

Brothers William and James Conway opened the first Mister Softee® in 1956. William served during WWII in the Navy. James served in the Navy during the Korean War. Mister Softee is operated exclusively from trucks. They list 350 franchises in 18 states on their website.[40]

1957 was the year of the WWII naval aviator for two big names in franchising.

Enterprise® Rentals was founded by Jack Taylor, a WWII fighter pilot, naming the company after the ship he served on, the USS *Enterprise*.[41] Enterprise has approximately 9,500 locations worldwide. They now only franchise outside the U.S.[42] Taylor's son, Andrew, while not a veteran, did go on to launch Alamo® and National® Car Rental. But it all started with Jack!

1957 also brought us the launch of what would become the Hyatt® Hotel chain, courtesy of Jay Pritzker, another naval aviator in WWII.[43] Hyatt has more than 1,300 locations worldwide.[44]

Robert Wildman served in the Army in WWII. In 1957, Wildman, along with his partners Frank and Donald Thomas, opened the first Burger Chef®. At its peak, Burger Chef had approximately 650 outlets. After a series of sales and acquisitions, the brand eventually died off.[45]

1958 was another very big year for veteran founders. Al Lapin, founder of International House of Pancakes® (now IHOP®) served in WWII.[46] His brother, Jerry Lapin, served during the Korean War and was awarded the Bronze Star, Silver Star, and Purple Heart.[47] IHOP has over 1,700 locations in 13 countries, starting with their first restaurant in 1958.[48]

Matt and Ivan Perkins opened the very first Perkins® Restaurant and Bakery in 1958. Matt served in the Army during WWII. Perkins has approximately 300 locations.[49]

Morris Mirkin served in the Army Air Forces during WWII. He opened the first Budget® Rent-a-Car in Los Angeles in 1958.[50] Budget claims approximately 2,700 locations on its website.

1958 also saw the launch of the first Pizza Hut® by brothers Frank and Dan Carney in Wichita, Kansas.[51] It appears Frank served in the Kansas National Guard, though documenting that took a bit of circumstantial evidence to pin down. Frank Carney sold his interests in Pizza Hut and became one of the largest franchisees of Papa John's® with 133 locations. His move to Papa John's upset a lot of folks at Pizza Hut at the time. Pizza Hut now has approximately 20,000 locations around the world.

John Bender, Air Force veteran and friend of the Carneys, created the original Pizza Hut pizza recipe, but his partnership with the Carneys was short-lived. The very first Pizza Hut franchise was sold to Dick Hassur, a friend of the Carneys. Hassur went on to own 150 Pizza Huts.[52] He served in the Army during the Korean War.

In 1972, PepsiCo® acquired Pizza Hut and later KFC, Taco Bell, and Long John Silver's®; all started by veterans, including Pepsi®! That's right, Pepsi-Cola was developed in 1893 by Caleb Bradham (he first called it Brad's Drink), who went on to be a Rear Admiral in the North Carolina Naval Militia. Pepsi uses the franchise model to distribute its products. As of February of 2025, PepsiCo has a market capitalization of over $200 billion.[53]

While we are at it, Coca-Cola® was invented by John S. Pembleton who was a Confederate soldier before he invented what we now call Coke®, for short. He began using the franchise model in 1889.[54] Confederate soldiers were never bestowed the status of veteran, but I thought it was worth a mention to show readers that Coca-Cola also uses the franchise model.

Jim Patterson may be the most prolific veteran franchise operator I've encountered. Patterson, a former Air Force officer, began his franchise journey as a franchisee of a coffee franchise operating under the name Jerry's®. Patterson admitted to almost giving up "in despair" several times as a franchisee (not uncommon and a good lesson for all of us). He grew his coffee "empire" to three locations in eight years, then decided to attempt what Kentucky Fried Chicken did, except in the fried fish space, under the name Long John Silver's®. Patterson sold his interests in Long John Silver's in 1975 and returned to being a franchisee, this time with Wendy's (47 units). During the 1980s he founded Rally's® Hamburgers (which later merged with Checkers®), helped launch Chi-Chi's® Mexican Restaurants (only one remains), and launched several other large non-franchise businesses.[55]

Mike Ilitch served four years in the Marines and went on to found Little Caesars® Pizza in 1959. Known as "Mister I," Ilitch, a former minor-league baseball player, later became owner of the Detroit Red Wings®. Little Caesars has approximately 4,200 locations.[56] An interesting fact I learned about Ilitch: When he learned Rosa Parks was assaulted and robbed, he paid to move her to a better apartment and quietly covered her rent. This only came to light after his passing in 2017.

The 1960s saw another batch of new franchise brands as well as the acceleration of growth from the brands launched in the 1950s.

Domino's Pizza founder, Tom Monaghan, thought he was enlisting in the Army but wound up in the Marines.[57] When you think about it, that is the most Marine thing a Marine could ever do. There are over 20,000

Domino's Pizza locations in the world after opening their first shop in 1960.[58]

Hardee's founder, Wilber Hardee, served in the Navy during WWII. Opened in 1960, they now have over 1,800 locations.[59] Stories vary, but Hardee either lost controlling interest in his company in a poker game or was allegedly swindled by his partners. In either case, he never got to enjoy the success of his namesake restaurant. He later rebounded from this setback and went on to become quite successful in other ventures.

The "Bell" in Taco Bell® comes from its founder, Glen Bell, a cook in the Marines during WWII. First opened in 1962, there are now approximately 7,000 Taco Bell locations in the world.[60]

Dave Drum, John Wallace, and two other partners founded KOA® Campgrounds in 1962. Drum earned a Purple Heart as a Marine in WWII and served again in the Korean War. He was described as a "cowboy with an IQ of 180." KOA now lists over 500 locations on their website.[61]

1962 also saw the launch of Motel 6® by William Becker, a WWII Navy veteran. The "6" in Motel 6 was chosen because that's the price he charged for rooms back when he started. Motel 6 has more than 1,400 locations in the U.S. and Canada.[62]

Television celebrity and Army veteran Dan Blocker launched the Bonanza® Steakhouse in 1963. Blocker played "Hoss" Cartwright on the TV show *Bonanza*. There was also another steakhouse franchise spinoff, Ponderosa®, from the series using the show's setting, the Ponderosa Ranch. Blocker sold out three years later to Sam Wyly, an Air Force veteran, and his brother, Charles. The brothers grew the brand to 600 locations and sold it in 1989. Wyly was on Forbes' list of the richest Americans in 2000 with a net worth of $750 million. Wyly got in all sorts of trouble with varying agencies over the years, including the IRS. He lost most of his wealth due to legal troubles.[63] Note to self: When I make my first billion, remember to pay the taxes.

One more odd fact I learned about the Wyly brothers—they donated to Swift Boat Veterans for Truth to attack John Kerry, a Vietnam veteran running for President.

Fred Rosati, WWII Army veteran, launched Rosati's® Pizza in 1964.[64] I get their "tavern style" pizza (the true Chicago style pizza) when I visit my brother in Evanston, Illinois. They have about 200 locations, mostly in Illinois.

Norman Brinker, Navy veteran, opened the first Steak and Ale® in 1966 after several years of working with Jack in the Box. At its height, Steak and Ale had 280 locations, according to Wikipedia. It was acquired by a company that eventually went bankrupt. Mr. Brinker's "fingerprints" are all over the restaurant franchise space as he trained and mentored many who went on to manage such brands as Chili's®, Applebee's®, TGI Fridays®, Boston Market®, Lettuce Entertain You®, and Sizzler®.[65] He is often credited with creating casual dining.

Econo-Travel® (later Econo Lodge®) launched in 1967 by Navy Korean War veteran Lloyd Tarbutton, with co-founders Vernon Myers and his son, Vernon Myers Jr. Econo Lodge now has over 800 locations in the U.S. and abroad.[66]

Two years later, Ed Hackbarth and David Jameson opened the first Casa Del Taco®. The name was later shortened to Del Taco®. Hackbarth was an Air Force veteran. Hackbarth first got his start with Glenn Bell in 1954 when Bell was running Bell's Burgers (before he launched Taco Bell). Del Taco has approximately 600 locations, the majority of which are in California.[67]

Brothers Forrest "Fuzzy" and Leroy Raffel founded Arby's in 1964. Both served—Fuzzy in the Army Air Forces and Leroy in the Naval Reserve during WWII. Arby's has over 3,500 restaurants in nine countries.[68]

Dollar A Day Rent A Car first launched in 1965 by founder Henry Caruso. Caruso joined the Navy as a pilot and served during WWII.

Dollar® Car Rental, as we know it today, has 570 locations worldwide.[69]

Ted and Doris Isaacson started their painting company, Servpro®, in 1967. Servpro evolved into a restoration business that now has over 1,700 locations. Ted served in the Army during the Korean War.[70]

1967 also brought us the first Kwik Kopy®, founded by Bud Hadfield, a Merchant Marine during WWII. Bud launched Kwik Kopy after failing previously at nine diverse businesses. He also launched AWT®, The Ink Well®, Franklin's Printing®, Kwik Kopy Business Centers, Parcel Plus®, and Computer Explorers®, each with varying degrees of success.[71]

Floyd "Sonny" Tillman and his wife, Lucille, opened their first Sonny's® Real Pit Bar-B-Q in 1968 and began franchising in 1977. Sonny enlisted in the Navy when he was just a sophomore in high school. Sonny's now has approximately 100 locations.[72]

The legendary Dave Thomas of Wendy's, who named his restaurant after his freckle-faced daughter, enlisted in the Army during the Korean War, and served in Germany. Having prior food production and service experience, Dave volunteered for the Cooks and Bakers School at Fort Benning. Wendy's has over 6,500 locations in 29 countries after breaking ground on their first store in 1969.[73]

Taco John's was created by John Turner in 1969. John served in the Air Force during the Korean War. Turner partnered with Harold Holmes (Army Air Forces WWII) and Jim Woodson, who also served in WWII (no branch given). The chain now boasts nearly 350 locations in 22 states.[74]

I mentioned Century 21 earlier in my discussion about conversion franchising. One of the co-founders, Marsh Fisher, was a B-25 bomber pilot with the U.S. Army Air Forces from 1943 to 1945.[75] Century 21 began in 1971 and now has approximately 14,000 independently owned and operated franchised broker offices in 86 countries and territories with over 147,000 sales agents.[76]

Raymond L. Danner Sr., an Army Air Corps veteran, founded Mr. D's Seafood and Hamburgers in 1969 (what we know today as Captain D's®). He also owned seven Shoney's® franchises and 22 Kentucky Fried Chicken outlets. In 1969 he took his company public and, two years later, merged his Shoney's interests with those of the chairman of Shoney's. Taking over as the new chairman, Danner oversaw 500 restaurants. At its peak, Shoney's had 1,600 stores generating $800 million in sales. Shoney's now has just 58 locations, but Captain D's has fared better with over 540 locations today.[77]

Dave Liniger, founder of RE/MAX®, enlisted in the Air Force and served in Vietnam. RE/MAX has grown to over 1,000 locations since its founding in 1973.[78] Liniger, 79, is still active in franchising with an acquisition of the Port of Subs® franchise by his Area 15 Ventures business. Port of Subs lists more than 135 locations on its website.

1974 brings us Incredible Sam's® by way of Sam Ross, a Navy veteran. He changed the name to Fantastic Sams® and began franchising in 1976. They have over 500 locations.[79]

Established in 1981 by Don Dwyer, Army veteran (mentioned throughout this book), Rainbow Carpet Cleaning and Restoration® now has over 400 locations worldwide. Dwyer went on to form the Dwyer Group which later became Neighborly, the largest home services franchise brand in the world.

1991 brings us Jan-Pro®, founded by Jacques Lapointe, one of the largest commercial cleaning franchises in the U.S., with roughly 10,000 franchises including Canada. Lapointe is an Army veteran.[80]

Ed Pendarvis founded Sunbelt® Business Brokers in 1993. Ed attended school at The Citadel and served two years in the Army Infantry. Sunbelt has approximately 250 licensed offices worldwide.[81]

As I mentioned earlier, Gordon Logan, former C-130 Air Force pilot, launched Sport Clips in 1993. 1,900 locations.

NOTE

This is the most comprehensive list I could come up with without using PhD interns to assist me. I'm certain I've over-looked many other veterans in the franchise space. Hopefully I can get a more fulsome list for the second edition of the book.

While not all of the roughly 300,000 locations listed above are owned by franchisees (many are company-owned), these companies would be mere shadows of their current state without the power of franchising.

There's also no telling how many thousands of these franchise locations are veteran-owned. Layer on top of that how many veterans have worked at these franchises over the decades and the impact from and for veterans is staggering.

I'd go so far as to say that without veterans, franchising, the way all goods and services are delivered around the globe, and our economy at large, would be a fraction of its current size.

Not even close.

Why Franchisors Want Veterans

The U.S. Army Leadership Field Manual identifies four features of an effective leader: values, attributes, skills, and actions.

Be. Know. Do.

To achieve excellence, each feature is further broken down:

- VALUES: loyalty, duty, respect, honor, integrity, personal courage, selfless service.
- ATTRIBUTES: self-discipline, initiative, self-confidence, professional bearing, physical fitness, emotional balance, and stability.
- SKILLS: interpersonal (teach, motivate, empower), conceptual (judgment, creative, ethical, critical thinking),

technical (job related, expertise), tactical (how to deploy assets).

- ACTIONS: influence others, get the job done on time and to standard, strive to improve.

Whether you served in a leadership position or not, we all reported to a leader a step above us. We know these attributes, these skills, these values as surely as we know ourselves. They form the core of military service regardless of your branch or rank.

Because of this, veterans are a target demographic for franchisors. They are betting the tenets of your military service will make you a strong franchise owner.

They aren't wrong.

While VetFran has been around since 1991, it's my observation the franchise world really started waking up to the true value of today's veterans in the early 2000s. That's when I noticed veteran recruitment into the franchise world really began to take off.

Military Experience Is Process Experience

Military service places you in a position of trusting the chain of command, trusting the system and your team to achieve the designated goal.

When you boil it down to the basics, franchises are really just systems. The franchisor develops the systems and the franchisees execute.

Rinse and repeat.

You bring your military experience to any franchise brand and they have already made positive assumptions about your ability to succeed within their system. That may or may not be wise on their part (there's more to being a great franchise owner than simply being a veteran), but it is an undeniable feature of your service: Franchisors see veterans as having the right mindset to succeed within their brands, to follow the systems. In other words, *The Right Stuff.*

There are two additional vital components in your military service that make you an attractive prospect for franchisors: accountability and perseverance.

At every step in your service you were held accountable to your platoon, fire team, squadron, command, or air wing. It was a fact of life in the service. Franchisors are looking to vet their prospects as surely as you are vetting them. One of the key components for a franchisor is how comfortable they are with their judgment of your accountability. Your franchise agreement lays out everyone's responsibilities, but franchisors don't want to be in the business of enforcing agreements. They want accountability. They want individuals who will be responsible for that accountability without hand-holding.

WARNING

If you find the franchisor is not vetting you and merely focuses on your ability to sign your franchise agreement and fund it, run away. They're merely interested in selling new franchises.

Beyond familiarity with processes, systems, teamwork, and accountability, one of the other more important attributes veterans bring to the table is perseverance.

The ability to get the job done when the sun is shining and there's a cool breeze is one thing. The ability to get it done in difficult or adverse conditions is another.

Improvise, adapt, and overcome, right?

Franchises are businesses, and all businesses have their challenges, opportunities, setbacks, and breakthroughs. A franchisor is trying to gauge whether or not any of their prospects will be able to persevere when the going gets tough. Because you are a veteran, that is a baked-in assumption.

Taking Veteran Recruitment Too Far

With all the competition for veterans, I'm seeing some over the top messaging being directed at our community that needs to be reeled in. Every one of those 4,000-ish franchises wants you. Some push a little too hard. For example, some broker websites go so far as to give the appearance of being official sites for veterans. Be certain you know the difference between shit and Shinola®.

NOTE

The expression *doesn't know shit from Shinola* gets its roots from WWII. Shinola was a popular black shoe polish used by the troops to keep their boots shined. It was considered mission critical to know the difference between the two (wink). Navin Johnson (Steve Martin) gets a lesson from his dad about knowing the difference between the two in one of my favorite movies, *The Jerk*, and it goes as you would expect (Navin steps in it). Shinola® was recently resurrected as a watch brand based in Detroit. BTW, I love my Shinola watches!

My message here is simply to beware if you see an overabundance of "patriotism" being thrown at you. There's also way too much "borrowed valor" being thrown around—where others use your service for their own means.

Up Next

In the next chapter, I'll describe some of the myths surrounding franchising and offer you a reality check on what you're getting into. After that, I'll run down how to vet a franchisor. Some of what was described above will come back into focus as part of your responsibility to do thorough due diligence before you sign anything.

Let's keep going.

CHAPTER 5

FRANCHISING MYTHS

When you start investigating the opportunities in franchising you will be met with a handful of ideas that, unchecked and unconsidered, hold the ability to wrongly influence you. You'll hear them in sales pitches. You'll subconsciously bring them with you, not knowing how prejudicial these ideas are. You'll encounter them on social media as everyone curates the experience they want to create for your consumption (whether it's real or not). These ideas are the root of bad decisions some people make when signing up for a franchise. Let's take a minute to go through them and defang them.

The Five Primary Franchising Myths are:

- Myth 1: Plug and Play/Business in a Box
- Myth 2: Autonomy
- Myth 3: Franchises are sure things, all but guaranteed
- Myth 4: Marketing and growth strategies are entirely the franchisor's responsibility
- Myth 5: Because you like a product or service means the franchise is a good fit

The surest way to give yourself the best chance to make an informed decision about whether or not franchising is for you and, if so, what type of franchise will best suit your needs, is to resist the lure of these myths. It can be hard to let go of ingrained assumptions; harder still if someone is selling you on a proposition you might have an unconscious internal bias toward, rather than the proposition selling itself.

This step is part of your due diligence.

With yourself.

This Field Manual also aims to help you look outside yourself, at what is offered, and how the processes work. As you go through this chapter, see how pervasive these myths have been in your own experience.

Myth 1: Plug and Play/Business in a Box

This is the most insidious of the myths. It is a promise made that cannot be kept. The very form of franchising precludes it, yet some prospective franchise owners are told, or assume, or some combination of the two, the franchise model is something that runs itself.

Nothing is further from the truth.

The basic premise of franchising is that you are buying into a proven system: systems tested and refined so that franchise owners can step into business without starting from zero.

It is from this the Myth of Plug and Play is born.

Franchises are extraordinary vehicles for entrepreneurship. Executed properly, they create a controlled risk mechanism through systems and processes properly tested in the market.

They are never a "no risk" system.

Sales pitches and individual assumptions take the act of buying into a system and equate it with the system doing the work. This is a misguided understanding of franchises and the obligations inherent in any franchise agreement.

The Oxford Dictionary defines entrepreneurship as "the activity of making money by starting or running businesses, especially when this involves taking financial risks; the ability to do this."

Entrepreneurs act, start, run, operate, make, and take risks. While a franchisor has taken on the risks to start and develop a successful business system, each franchise owner is required to do the same with their business. To assume once you've paid the fees the business will function on its own because of others' previous efforts is to doom your investment.

Franchise owners are required to bring diligence, effort, and personal accountability to bear—the very traits that make veterans a desirable target for franchise sales. Consider it a red flag, a monstrous red flag, if you hear from a broker or company rep that any franchise operation is a business in a box and all you have to do is turn on the lights.

That franchise does not exist. Some might get a little close to that, but not many. And those are meant for the heavy hitters with deep pockets and staff.

If you are buying a franchise as an owner-operator, then you are fully aware that you are the one who will put in the work. If you are buying into a model where you, as the franchise owner, build the team that will execute, you are still engaged in managing your crews and managers. There is no scenario where your hand is not on the tiller. You've "got the conn," as they say in the Navy.

Franchising is all about systems that work. But, you have to work the system.

Be clear about that from the start and you will avoid disappointment and financial losses down the road.

Myth 2: Autonomy

This next myth is an overcorrection to the first one. I just argued there is no plug and play. Franchisors need franchise owners: people willing to commit time, effort, capital, and their own integrity to the success of the franchise. That is completely true. However, sometimes franchise owners, whether they are a top achiever, or somewhere down the line, come to see themselves as separate and distinct from the brand they've bought into.

Franchising is not a binary code. It isn't all up to the brand, nor is it all up to the franchisee to find, build, and grow markets. It is a relationship that is defined by the franchise agreement (and disclosed in the FDD), and any attempts to operate in contradiction to the brand standards cannot be tolerated.

Sounds harsh but let me explain why this is a good thing.

A good franchisor builds a business system, tests it, proves it in the market, and offers units for sale through their FDD, consummated with a franchise agreement. The systems and processes need to be replicable. The franchisor needs to provide training on those processes so everyone in the system knows how to operate it. So far, all of the risk and costs are the franchisor's. When units are sold, those franchise partners are obligated under the terms of the franchise agreement to operate their businesses in a specific, conditional manner. That's the deal you strike.

Some think themselves not bound by these limits. They know better, have better ideas, or simply disdain any boundaries. Even if they bring in a great deal of revenue, this is a disaster for the franchisor and the brand at large. The brand cannot be sustained with rogue operators. Rogue operators hurt not only the franchisor, they can also do even greater harm to fellow franchisees.

Your success in any franchise is determined by the research you put in up front, the unit(s) you buy and their market(s), and the direct effort you put into your business. All of that happens within a prescribed network of relationships between yourself, the corporate team, fellow franchisees, approved vendors, and others you have orbiting your business (coaches and mentors, etc.).

You are never alone. That's one of franchising's greatest appeals. To act as if you were different from that network will only cause untenable friction. No system will tolerate for very long a threat to the whole.

To buy into a franchise system you are opting into several relationships that are not optional and cannot be ignored. Yes, there are contracts and lawyers involved and when push comes to shove those contracts will be enforced. But if you know yourself to be one who does not want to have any limits placed on you, then franchising is simply not for you. Remember, the reason for looking into franchises is to find the right mix of opportunity and support in order to be successful.

There are no cowboys or cowgirls here. Make sure you understand you.

Myth 3: Franchises Are Sure Things, All but Guaranteed

Inaccurate statistics about franchise industry success rates are all over the internet. Some years back, the U.S. Department of Commerce published a survey (not a study) in the 1980s claiming a 95% success rate for franchises. It became affectionately known as "The Stat."

Unfortunately, it was a highly flawed survey. Nevertheless, it became the statistic brokers and franchisors used to pitch franchises versus going it alone. The IFA formally distanced themselves from this statistic in 2005. You can still find this 95% success rate floating around in the ether and on franchise websites.

Ignore that number. It's almost meaningless anyway. You need to determine the probable success rate of the franchise you are looking to join, not some number about the industry itself.

There Are No Guarantees

Franchisors have devoted time and resources building, testing, and honing the concept and its processes. A lot of guesswork has been handled and countless mistakes have been made so you don't have to make those same mistakes. When you buy in, you are stepping into systems that have had a lot of attention and achieved specific results (which always need confirming by you).

None of that guarantees your success. There is no guarantee in any entrepreneurial effort. It is the nature of entrepreneurship to take risks. It is important to know where risk can come from with franchising. There are at least four primary risks that you need to be aware of:

- Macro-economic change
- The micro-economics of your unit/territory
- Corporate failure to execute
- Individual failure to execute the plan

Macro-economics

There are almost 4,000 active franchise concepts available in the United States and countless others considered inactive, as they are no longer actively pursuing franchise sales. Not all of them are successful, and finding the right match to your expectations and skills is just the beginning of your work.

You can do everything right. You can find a great organization that you want to work with—one that respects what you bring to them, to their brand. But, there are forces that you cannot control as a franchise owner which can impact your ability to operate your business. Recessions (some brands flourish in recessions), a tight money market, international affairs, local environmental issues, employee shortages, pandemics, etc., all can weigh on any entrepreneurial effort. Franchising gives you some cover from these events, but if any crisis extends itself for a length of time, it could affect your bottom line. Franchises are not, in and of themselves, immune.

Micro-economics

This should be part of your deliberations: What is the size of the territory you are buying into? How saturated is it with competition? What is the price point in your area versus other parts of the system? Are there larger economic impacts? How is that experienced in your territory?

You may find a low cost opportunity within home services to serve a large suburban area, but if it is oversold with competitors, or worse, oversold by the franchisor, what are you buying into, exactly? Can you compete? Always look for apples to apples when comparing territories: population, maturation of market, number of competitors, demographics, average home values, etc. The franchisor should be able to articulate why they think your chosen territory will work.

Corporate (Franchisor) Failure

This one is painful. You are buying into someone else's dream and system. They have a duty to reveal their turnover rate, the lawsuits that may be attached to them, bankruptcies, and other ugly business realities in the FDD.

You might wish to do a search for "Anchored Tiny Homes franchise" to witness the collapse of a brand that likely got caught up in the tiny home frenzy but couldn't make it work. Ouch.

Lawsuits can be a red flag. Anyone can sue anyone for anything—it's America! Sometimes the franchisor could be drawn into a legal battle they don't deserve. Ask hard questions about litigation listed in the FDD or any you found via online sleuthing. Don't let them hide behind a political style response such as "We can't comment . . ." They can absolutely state the allegations and their response. You can also call the opposing parties to see what they say. But, don't let one disgruntled franchisee scare you away. It's sometimes impossible to make two people happy, let alone dozens, or hundreds, or thousands. Most lawsuits are a matter of open public record. Also discuss any litigation issues with your franchise attorney for their take on it.

On the other side of that coin I have seen some pretty litigious franchisors chasing folks for money who tried their best but simply had their businesses fail. Then, the franchisor makes matters worse by attempting to collect on liquidated damages or other remedies found in their franchise agreement. This behavior, while typically within their legal rights, would fall outside what is now called Responsible Franchising, a recent and welcome initiative within the franchise industry, discussed later.

Alternatively, the franchisor might well be deserving of legal action. Conduct an internet search for "BurgerIM franchise." In any multi-billion-dollar industry you will find bad actors. My hope is to give you enough tools to help you avoid them.

As with most things, it's all relative. When a franchise brand has thousands of locations, its legal risks become exponential, and it would be almost unthinkable to find a brand of that scale without some sort of litigation. But if you've got a much smaller brand with even just one or a few lawsuits, what's up with that? Look closely. If you can't put all your legal concerns to rest at this stage, walk away.

A high turnover rate can be another red flag. I do not know of a hard number or percentage of what "bad" turnover is but, like Supreme Court Justice Potter Stewart once famously said about obscenity and pornography, "I know it when I see it." By the way, Justice Stewart served in the Navy Reserve during WWII and is buried in Arlington Cemetery.

A turnover/failure rate of 15% to 20% is probably less than ideal but might be acceptable. It depends. VetFran caps franchisors at 20% turnover to receive VetFran's highest ranking of five stars. Maybe anything over 20% to 25% is a big yellow caution light. 30% to 35% or more over the last three years? Something is really off. Proceed with utmost skepticism.

Some location turnovers can also be a sign of a healthy brand. Franchise recruitment is a little like the *90 Day Fiancé* reality show. Wham. Bam. I like you. You like me. Let's do this!

Then the (real) reality sets in. Maybe the new franchise owner is not a good fit. What if they're causing problems? Getting in silly conflicts with vendors? Not following up with customers? Causing harm to the brand? Ask me how I know about this.

The franchisor needs a way to unwind the franchise agreement if the franchisee can't make a course correction. Hopefully, it's by mutual agreement and the franchise is sold or terminated amicably.

Should that be a ding on the franchisor? Maybe. Maybe the real criticism is they need to vet better. But the vetting process, no matter how stringent, is not infallible.

Individual Failure

Buy a great opportunity, a great system, a great brand with a high performing corporate team, and you can still fail. As Mav's back seater said in *Top Gun: Maverick,* "It's not the plane, it's the pilot."

You're the captain of your business.

Act like it.

Most franchises that go bust go bust because the effort was not put in to make it work. The system was ignored, or only partially implemented and partial results came out of that. I'm aware of one franchise brand with one franchisee doing $10 million in sales whose territory abuts another franchisee doing $100,000 in sales. A little tough to point the finger at the franchisor if you're the latter.

If you freeze up because you are overwhelmed, you can reach out to others for help when you belong to a franchise. If you simply don't put in the effort, no amount of support will save you. You needn't be the most skilled or the most proficient in order to succeed. But you do need to be the most open to learn and implement what you've learned.

No system is a sure thing. All systems are made up of people who do or don't give their full attention to the tasks at hand. Find a place you have confidence in, build relationships across the brand, and work at your work with all of your attention and care, and you stand a far better than average chance to succeed.

Myth 4: Marketing and Growth Strategies Are Entirely the Franchisor's Responsibility

One of the reasons you buy into a franchise is because of the brand. You are paying a premium for not only a proven business model (there's that word "proven" again) but also an established brand. The franchisor is responsible for cultivating the brand's presence and reputation nationally/regionally. It is the franchisee's responsibility to uphold the brand's reputation and cultivate the brand and their own unit's reputation in the local market.

Your franchisor should provide the umbrella marketing, the overarching message. If you simply point to that effort as the sum of what is required, your business won't flourish.

You will need to supplement the franchisor's marketing. Often, local franchisees do the lion's share of local marketing. A good franchisor will have systems in place to make this fairly easy. Hopefully, they've also got a marketing dashboard that tracks results. You just need to make sure the marketing efforts are executed and funded.

This goes back to the plug and play myth. Marketing is broadly driven by corporate efforts. That does not relieve you of your responsibility to engage in localized marketing efforts. Whether that is through your own robust social media presence (following brand guidelines), wrapping your vehicle(s) with brand graphics, sponsoring local events, joining the local chamber of commerce or other networking organizations, direct mail, radio, offering your goods and/or services to local charities, guerrilla marketing, or any other of the scores of opportunities that present themselves in your community, you are in charge of these efforts.

A failure to engage with this reality will hamper your ability to succeed.

Most franchises will require a certain level of spending at the unit level to market the brand. Know what your required ad spend is (it's listed in your FDD), recognize it might still not be enough to achieve the sales goals you desire, and be prepared to spend that money. I can't empha-size this enough. You've got to spend money to make money. Even with a franchise.

Ask lots of questions about the marketing piece.

Myth 5: Because You Like a Product or Service Means the Franchise Is a Good Fit

Like all consumers, you have interacted with franchises often, if not on a near daily basis. Probably way more often than you realize. I recently went to grab some food from a new pizza joint near me. Of the eight stores in this particular strip mall, seven were franchise brands. I had to do a quick internet search because most were brands I'd never heard of. Maybe some were from the 450 new franchise brands that launched in 2023.

I loved the pizza, but I have no idea if it's a good investment. It's a new franchise with two locations. If I were in the market for a food fran-chise to buy I'd definitely look into this brand. I'd want to be sure I'm looking at it the right way, not clouded by my personal desire to have easy access to great pizza, an admitted weakness of mine.

Like me and my love of pizza, there are some products and services that you really like. That's great. That's what franchisors are looking for in their markets: customer loyalty, brief cycle times, dollars being spent with them instead of someone else. This probably won't translate the way you think it might when it comes time to choose a franchise.

Your franchise investment is less about enthusiasm for a particular product or service and much more an enthusiasm for the business opportunity the franchise offers in delivering that product or service and creating the work-life balance you desire. Don't get me wrong, you need to be passionate about your deliverables and get it right, but the product itself may not necessarily be your primary threshold.

If I may, let's discuss parking lot striping. I can assure you that not one of our franchise partners ever, in their wildest dreams, woke up one day and said, "Honey, I really want to own a parking lot striping business!" Not one.

Despite some hurdles, we were able to get them to look past the type of service we offered and look more closely at the type of business opportunity offered to the veteran: an owner-operator model designed to transition to an owner-manager model, created specifically for today's veteran, with built-in camaraderie, in a niche market. And their own efforts can directly impact their bottom line. That pretty much sums up our Unique Selling Proposition (USP).

What's the USP for the brands you're looking into? They should have a compelling USP for you as a franchise prospect and they should also have a separate, very strong USP for the end customer as well.

I'm simply here to tell you that you should expand your search criteria and be open to concepts you might otherwise ignore at first blush. Does it matter if you've got crews striping parking lots, installing gutters, cleaning dryer vents, making donuts, cleaning windows, flipping burgers, painting houses, scooping ice cream, scooping dog poop, mowing lawns, killing mosquitoes, or even cleaning toilets, if running the business is your role? Which franchise can give you the ROI, work-life balance, and *sense of purpose* that you are seeking?

You are looking for opportunities to operate your own business—opportunities that have strong unit economics, a strong corporate team, a killer brand, and the chance to grow. Nowhere does it say you have to be passionate about donuts to buy into Dunkin'.

Franchises do require a passion for the business, for running it well, for serving your customers, for taking care of any staff you bring on, for mastering the skills needed to run the back of the house, and engaging with your marketing efforts. Don't confuse the love of something with making that a business opportunity to acquire.

Next up: How To Vet a Franchisor.

CHAPTER 6

HOW TO VET A FRANCHISOR

Throughout this book I am asking you to do a gut check at each and every step of the way. You have to pass muster with yourself, your intentions, your goals, and expectations. Doing so is one of the greatest predictors of future success. If you have properly vetted yourself before vetting these organizations, then the process of looking into the various franchise opportunities becomes clearer. None of this is a cakewalk. It requires your focused attention. Being clear-eyed at each step allows you the freedom to choose and choose wisely.

If you've passed your own reality check to this point, let's get started sorting through other factors you need to weigh in your search for a franchise fit. You have strategic choices to make.

This chapter will help you:

- Understand the leadership structure of any franchise-related organization: who the players are and what their expertise is.
- Know how to assess unit economics: territory size, scalability, and local competition.
- Understand how the corporate operations are run: training,

equipment, tech platforms, back of office systems, continuing education, coaching, mentorship, and access to support.

- Understand the growth opportunities at the unit level and multi-unit level: is the model clear, simple, and replicable?
- Recognize the best path to follow for a clean exit.
- Ask how the current corporate sales and marketing plans align with unit efforts: what's the reach and calendar, what platforms are being used?
- Prepare to review the FDD.

For now, take the widest possible view. There will be plenty of time to drill down into the specifics of a given opportunity. At this stage a broad understanding will help set up that more specific effort.

Let's go.

Gathering Intel on the Leadership and Structure

When you buy a franchise you are not only buying into a specific brand, but also entering into a relationship with those who operate and manage the brand. You need to take the time to understand who they are, what their experience is, and how they've organized the company.

There is plenty of useful information that can be pulled from the FDD, sales materials, and conversations you engage in. Once you have the names of the principals, you can look them up online. Be sure to include a search on LinkedIn. LinkedIn is a self-curated business-oriented social media platform. That means, for the most part, no one is vetting what's put on LinkedIn other than the authors.

Find the folks you want a little more background on via LinkedIn and view their profile. Hit "follow" and then view their posts and comments. Now you can read through what they have posted. You will learn their claimed educational background, work history, how they frame them-selves by the stories they tell, how they interact with others, and if they have been consistent in how they represent themselves over time.

What you sometimes encounter is a flooding of the zone with lots of rah-rah content. *LOTS*. If I gave you this simple quiz: *Can you trust everything on social media?* you'd get the answer correct, of course. *No!* But the subconscious can be more powerful than the conscious. Being bombarded with positive messaging can create false assumptions and you might begin developing a confirmation bias to sell yourself on a brand you find interesting.

I'm well aware of some brands that are really struggling yet present to the world that everything is hunky-dory via LinkedIn and other social media. Your job is to separate the wheat from the chaff (and the Shinola).

It isn't just LinkedIn, Instagram®, or Twitter® (it will always be Twitter to me), or any other social media space that you need to look into. It will come up again when I go through the FDD in the next chapter, but look for any news articles that mention the brand's principals or lawsuits they might be involved in. Try and gather information from somewhere other than the FDD. Search engines (Google®, Yahoo®, Bing®, ChatGPT®, etc.) are your friends. Search "[franchise brand] lawsuits," "[franchise brand] reviews," "[franchise brand] complaints," "[principal's name] lawsuits," etc. If the brand is part of an umbrella group, also do a search on that.

Finally, check out the Google reviews for local franchised units to see how the brand is functioning in practice around the country.

NOTE

This last step of checking franchisee reviews is often overlooked.

If you pick up any troubling info, don't be afraid to ask. There could be a mix-up (there's a billionaire out there somewhere with a similar name to mine who got into a little, shall we say, salacious trouble).

All of the above is critical. Just as important: Make sure you are given the time to speak directly with the principals. If everything is coming to you through a filter (a broker, say, or the second assistant to the assistant vice-president in charge of the runaround) ask why you can't get that critical access. Meeting someone face-to-face, even if only via an online video meeting in an obvious sales setting, is still an important step to take to help you gauge the organization.

Once you know the players, you need to understand the organization.

Are you looking at a brand with PE money behind it? Brands are sold and resold by PE as their investors are looking for a specific return within a specific time frame. Look at who is in place. Have they stayed through any brand sales, or is it a new team?

As one example, according to the *Franchise Times*,[1] Senior Helpers®, a senior care franchise, has changed hands four times with PE since its founding in 2004. Is that a bad thing? A good thing? That's not for me to judge. Sales are often just the way of business in the bigger money brands. Smaller brands don't generate the interest from PE. Again, is that good or bad? I'm not passing judgment either way. Just making you aware.

If PE is in involved, does the founder maintain a role? The CEO and co-founder of Senior Helpers, is still CEO despite the revolving door of PE.

You'll need to understand who your point of contact will be and any layers between them and the corporate officers if you become a franchisee. Who is in charge of training? Marketing? Franchise support? These are questions that aren't asked often enough. Don't be shy.

Go deep in these conversations whenever you can. It will help you gain valuable perspective on how issues are resolved, how innovations are incorporated, and how the organization prioritizes its comms throughout the system.

Unit Economics

When looking into which franchise opportunity is the best fit for you, understanding the unit economics is where all of your ideas about business ownership meet economic reality. There are several variables at play here. The most important thing you can do is to get as close as you can to true comparisons. No two franchise organizations are going to offer the exact same territories or have the same exact profit and loss and revenue statements. Keep in mind what your goals are throughout. Are you looking for side income, looking to give yourself a job, or are you looking to build generational wealth? That continuum of goals affects how you analyze the unit economics.

There are five general areas that you need to evaluate:

1) Demographics
A: How is the territory defined?
B: Is it scalable?
C: Who is the competition in the same area and how do they define their territories?
D: Within the brand, how do similar territories perform?

2) Revenue v. Profit and Loss

3) The Model
A: Is the model clear and replicable?
B: What are the economics for multi-unit franchisees?

4) Initial Investment and ROI
A: ITEM 19 in the FDD
B: History of break-even point within the system

5) Key Performance Indicators (KPIs)
A: Within the brand
B: Establishing KPIs

Demographics

When looking at how territories are defined, there are a host of ways it can be done: population, radius, percentage of homes valued at X or above, number of single-family homes, per capita income, etc. Most are typically bounded geographically in the service space, but the actual size in terms of square miles doesn't tell you the whole story. It must be said that, depending on the type of franchise you are buying (food service, home services, financial services, health care, personal care/fitness), there will be different pressures in play that make it irrelevant to compare across sectors. If you are looking at personal care/fitness operations, that has a different requirement than fast-food restaurants or professional services brands do. For our purposes here, I'm going to concentrate on mid- and lower-tier opportunities, so if you're looking to those larger, multi-unit and big name franchise investments, you'll need to search out a different guide.

The sector you are looking into will have its own unofficial matrix for determining how a territory is defined. One of the best ways to understand what you're looking at is to contact the competition and review their FDD. It should go without saying, but I'm going to say it anyway: Always check for franchise competitors and sign up to hear their pitch. Find a way to get to their FDDs. How are they carving up their territories and how does that compare to the opportunity you are looking into? Competitor FDDs can help you expand your knowledge of the industry and might even expose you to a better option.

We have snagged more than a few franchisees from our competitors. These prospects wisely did their due diligence for franchise comparisons and chose us because we offered a better deal economically—and because of our veteran mission.

Okay. Guilty. Minus two points for self-promotion. But those wins are particularly satisfying.

Back to comparisons and research. I would always suggest you look into competing brands, even if they are sold out in the desired territory.

Taking the extra step is what will help you find your entrepreneurial home.

If you are looking into a home services brand, knowing the number of homes and their value is essential. If you are looking at business services (printing, graphics, vehicle wraps, fleet washing, facility management) that's a different construct.

Next question: Is it scalable? First, it may not matter to you if the opportunity is scalable. About half of franchise owners have only one unit.[1] Your goals for supplemental income or giving yourself a job may preclude the need for scalability. If you are looking farther down the road, to build bigger generational wealth, then scalability matters.

Are there opportunities to take on more units? If so, where are they located? How complete is the brand's footprint in your area/region? If scalable, are you ready to manage multiple units? Hire others? Build teams? If this is your goal, then these questions have to be answered so you can determine your strategy for acquiring multiple units, operating them, and receiving the necessary support from the brand to do so.

If multiple units aren't your desired path, are add-on services an option within the brand? That's another way to increase revenue.

I mentioned above that a good way to know the score in terms of territory is to review your potential competition's FDD. That may not be possible, but it is worth a try. At a bare minimum, you need to know who you are competing with, how long they've been in the market, and their relative strength. If a competitor is struggling, is it because the market isn't buying, or has that operation failed to capitalize on its opportunities? Their FDD may hold some answers the first FDD doesn't.

One more thing to take into account: What is the performance of similar territories within the brand? You are looking for demographics similar to what is being offered to you. Contact those franchisees to get their take on what it was like coming on board, their business strategy, and if they've crossed their break-even point and are growing. It won't be a perfect match because A) you can't account for all demographics, and B) even if all things are equal, there is no way to control for individual effort—theirs or yours.

Are They Growing Internally?

This one might easily be overlooked. If nothing is there, how do you know something is missing? What I'm saying is an established franchise will show some internal growth if the franchisees are happy. If they aren't happy, you won't see any additional acquisition activity and may not realize what you're missing.

If, on the other hand, you're looking at a brand where franchisees are gobbling up more territories and/or locations, you may have just found yourself a winner.

Revenue v. Profit and Loss

ITEMS 19, 20, and 21 in the FDD are where franchisors make their financial claims, show unit growth or shrinkage (*not* the George Costanza kind), turnover, and recent corporate audits. We'll get to all that in the next chapter, but for now, know this information is provided to you as a means of transparency, albeit somewhat limited. If you don't know how to interpret the information, that transparency will be lost on you. The point here is to establish baseline information so you can assess what is presented.

NOTE

If the franchisor doesn't have an ITEM 19 (Financial Representations), they can't make any earnings claims to you whatsoever, nor can any broker. My franchise legal friends tell me terms like "highly profitable!" and "make great money!" in ads, emails, or sales pitches, all might be considered an earnings claim. While the franchisor/broker might be restricted from making an earnings claim, there is no prohibition for any current or former franchisee from sharing their numbers and profit or loss experience.

Use the franchisees, past and present, to your advantage.

To start, revenue is simply the amount of money generated from business activities before expenses are factored in. There are different formulas for expressing revenue: gross revenue, average revenue per unit, monthly recurring revenue, annual recurring revenue, and others. It is against these numbers that your expenses are deducted.

Revenue is the base of the pyramid. Expenses and per unit costs follow. Make sure your research reveals what you can expect in terms of ongoing investment beyond initial fees, and what the historical timeline has been for the brand and its locations to reach the top of the pyramid: profit.

The Model

The model presented to you not only has to answer your questions about the day in the life, investment, ROI, growth, and how all of that is held in the relationship with the brand, but you have to believe the system can be executed over and over by others.

Being part of a brand means you are somewhat tied to the performance of others within the brand, just as you are tied to the corporate team. A key indicator for success is how the systems are built. Is it like an EOD tech being given a hammer and a plumber's wrench? Or, are the lines of operation clear and straightforward?

It can be argued that any model can be improved and adjusted over time. That's fine, but you aren't looking for perfect. You are looking for clean, clear, understandable, and replicable so when you scale up, or sell it off, there is as little friction as possible because the model works. The model needs to work and work every time someone commits to its success.

How do you determine if what you're looking at is a strong brand? There should be a history of success in the FDD, not a history of chaotic turnover, and the franchisees you contact are eager to talk about their excitement for the brand. It's sometimes that simple.

Initial Investment and ROI

We touched on this above, but I want to take a minute to talk about initial investment and its weight on ROI. Your franchise fee and the initial costs of buying in are determined by several factors including, but not limited to, the success, reach, and history of the franchise. It is based on the demographics of the territory, and it factors in broker commissions and any offered discounts (i.e., military discounts, early adopter discounts, etc.). The franchise fee can never be inconsistent across a brand—there's not supposed to be a friends and family discount that favors unspecified populations. Because brokers' commissions are often 50% or higher, franchisors factor that into their offer. Even if you work directly with the franchisor without the broker the franchise fee should be the same.

Beyond the franchise fee, you will likely have required equipment and/or products to acquire in addition to all your back-office and other overhead costs. Lease? Buildout? Staff? Each sector where franchising operates is different and requires different things from its franchisees. Be clear-eyed from the start. You want to know your total initial expenditures before you sign anything. You will have ongoing costs as well. This affects your financing options and your break-even point—that moment where you can start feeling the return on your investment.

Key Performance Indicators (KPIs)

KPIs vary across sectors. Some KPIs are straightforward: total sales, average sales, gross margin, cost of goods sold, closure rate, sales growth rate, repeat customer rate, and time to breakeven. You'll want to hear from current franchisees what they're experiencing. That can feel intrusive to them. Build some rapport well before you tackle questions like that.

There is one more essential KPI for your search that should be less intrusive: the basic measure of franchisee satisfaction. You'll learn pretty quickly where each franchisee stands if you can engage them on a phone call or site visit. Joe Mathews of The Franchise Performance Group, a 40-year veteran of franchising, claims franchise brands must have a Net Promoter Score of 80% or higher on this one question: "Would you do it again?" (buy this franchise).

NOTE

A Net Promoter Score is a measure of customer loyalty. In this case the "customer" is the franchisee.

Corporate Operations

When you sign up for a brand, you are buying into that brand's corporate operations. The brand is more than sales and marketing. It is operational.

Brands that prioritize franchise sales growth strategies over supporting their existing franchisees must be avoided. Existing franchisees will know the score.

As part of the vetting process of any organization you are considering, take the time to understand its corporate structure as it relates to operations:

- Who is in charge of the onboarding process?
- Where is training conducted? By whom? Is it on specific equipment? What about back office training?
- Is there a defined support system with clear communication channels?
- What sort of access do you have to decision makers?

Every organization will build out their corporate operations team differently. Ask if an FSO is handling these tasks or is it still in the hands of the founder's team? Has dedicated staff been brought on for these issues or are a few people multitasking? The answers will likely differ, and you will have to decide if the answers comport with your expectations but, make no mistake, every organization needs to have answers for these questions.

Branding Is Everything

The brand itself is your first line of marketing. You've heard the phrase "building your brand" as it relates to your career and industry presence. It is that on steroids for franchisors.

Franchisors bear the cost and effort to develop not only the graphics, the content, and the system itself, they also leverage all of that into brand awareness, presence and, through all that, trust. The work of brand management goes far beyond just advertising. It goes beyond a web presence. It is the business itself, and as a franchisee you have a role to play in maintaining and furthering that cause.

Sales and Marketing

Set aside for now the requirements of the franchisor to build their brand. Franchise agreements will likely stipulate a minimum marketing budget from each franchise location. Depending on the franchise you buy into, that could mean hundreds of dollars a month, thousands, or many thousands. If you sit back and rely solely on company-generated leads or company-generated marketing efforts, you will a) leave money on the table, b) single yourself out within the system as someone who drafts off others' work, c) be a weak link, and d) lag in sales. Your business is more than your labor and more than managing your team. It is growing your franchise into an integral part of the communities you serve.

Boots on the ground branding/marketing is what drives sales for many systems. The franchisor gets you inside the red zone. You have to punch it in. Below is a partial list of ways you may be tasked with either funding and/or participating in:

- Social media ad buys
- Trade shows
- Trade magazine ad buys
- Networking groups
- Targeted mailers/flyers
- Team sponsorships
- Charity event sponsor
- YouTube ads and/or videos (highlighting the business, employees, customers)
- Strong LinkedIn presence (to attract attention to the work)
- Sales promos

Your mileage will vary depending on your industry, but the point here is that, as a franchisee, you hold the difference makers in your hands. The best marketing is to do your work and do it well to generate word-of-mouth sales. But that won't be enough. You have to get comfortable with the idea that, while you have the support from the corporate office, the success of your franchise is dependent on the things you think, say, and do to let others know about your business.

NOTE

Here's a hint on being a good franchise partner. If the franchisor tells you they haven't had luck with certain platforms (maybe Angi®, Yelp®, Facebook® ads), don't try to reinvent the wheel. Most franchisors have made countless mistakes so you don't have to. If you insist on trying avenues they don't recommend, please do so using additional funds, not the funds that were supposed to be used on approved channels. Other tips on being a great franchisee are found in Appendix 1.

You should expect a robust marketing plan from the brand. You should expect to be given guidelines about how you are to use the corporate images. You should expect to be coached, advised, and encouraged to take control of much of your own marketing plan, using their guidelines. You should not expect corporate efforts to be the only thing you need to be successful (there are exceptions). It goes a long way, but each franchisee has a responsibility here. Keep this in mind as you close in on making a decision about buying a franchise. As a business owner, whether you have bought a franchise to give yourself a job or are committed to building out successful teams to run your operations, you will be keeping owner hours. That's not happy hour at the NCO Club. It is putting the necessary time and thought into how you will deploy the marketing materials and budget available to you.

Franchisors Are Bridges

My franchise colleague and Marine veteran, Joshua Emison, likes to use a bridge analogy for franchisors.

You (the new franchisee) are standing on one side of the canyon (your franchise start-up), and you need to get to the other side (profitability, work/life balance, and your definition of success).

In between is the franchisor (the bridge). Your job is to find the largest bridge that can help you close that gap. The wider the bridge, the less you have to build on your own.

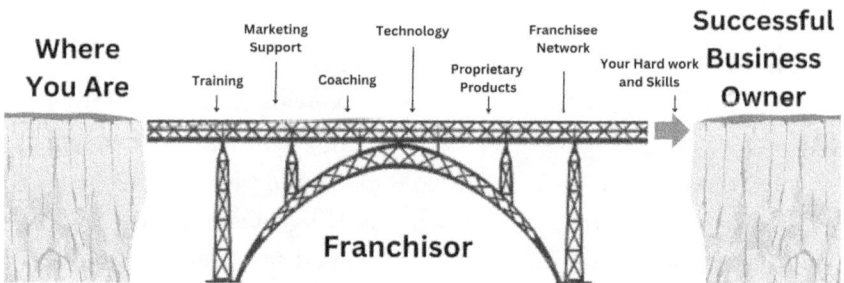

Credit: Joshua Emison

I love this analogy.

Thanks, Josh, for letting me use it.

All of the above are for you to consider as you weigh the opportunities in front of you. Your broker/franchise rep should have more to add, but this gives you a broad view of the things to look for and to keep in mind as you consider your options. What were once possible contingencies become your responsibilities when the ink dries.

This is your future. Take the time to understand as much as you can. In the next chapter I'll go line by line through all 23 items in the FDD and let you know what those items entail and where the story of the franchisor is told. It's not legal advice. It is just the view from someone on the inside, someone who is biased in favor of my fellow vets.

CHAPTER 7

HOW TO READ THE FDD

Receiving the FDD

Franchisors vary on when they present you with their FDD. You must have the FDD at least 14 days before signing any franchise agreement. Typically you'll need to be screened at least a little bit before they release their FDD. Capital-intensive franchise systems will usually perform heavier financial pre-screening before they give you much of their time.

FDDs are mandated legal documents that have a story to tell if you know how to read them. Your franchise attorney will be your primary professional resource in reviewing these documents. It is critical that you have some understanding and awareness of the information they contain instead of simply signing off on a stack of papers. You must read the FDD and ask questions for clarification.

FDDs have a very strict and standardized format. All FDDs have a cover page with other general information, followed by 23 very specific items. Most franchisors will also send you a copy of their sample franchise agreement along with their FDD so you may see an example of what you'd be signing if you join the brand. Essentially, the franchise agreement codifies what is disclosed in the FDD into contract language.

NOTE

Most franchisors will require an application or some sort of dialogue before they'll send you their FDD. Highly sophisticated (expensive) brands will require a fair amount of pre-qualification before they start sending out FDDs or spending a lot of time with you (think big name fast food, hotel chains, and others like that). Anecdotally, financial pre-qualification tends to run parallel to the dollar amounts involved. You might also be able to find the FDD for a brand you're interested in without an application or even speaking with a representative via some online sleuthing.

Four states offer a free FDD lookup for franchises that have registered in those states. That means they won't have the FDD you're looking for if that brand didn't file with that state.

California

Indiana

Minnesota

Wisconsin

Conduct an internet search for "[state listed above] franchise disclosure documents."

FranChimp has a pretty extensive list of franchises and FDDs on file. Visit FranChimp.com and enter the brand name in the search box at the top. Not all brands are listed here, either. There is a cost for each brand's FDD.

VettedBiz.com has lots of resources for franchise prospects.

You might also try The FDD Exchange at FDDExchange.com. You may view one FDD per day for free or pay for more frequent access.

How I Read the FDD

I can't give legal advice, but I will tell you what I would look for in the FDD. As always, consult a qualified franchise attorney for legal guidance.

Once you have the FDD in hand, here's what I would recommend: Unless they snail mailed you one (I suppose someone might still be doing that), send your digital copy to a local print shop to have it printed and spiral bound. While you can read the FDD on your desktop, laptop, or even (shudder) your mobile device, I do not recommend these methods.

First, it's lengthy and hard to read digitally. Secondly, having that paper document in hand allows you to pick it up and read it easily. You can then make notes in the margins, circle, or underscore items you wish to explore further, dog-ear certain pages, etc. You now have these live notes handy when you visit with your franchise attorney and when you get into deeper discussions with the franchisor.

While some of the items in the FDD have greater importance, I think following the FDD from start to finish is a good way to digest it.

Every FDD follows the exact same format of ITEMS 1 through 23 plus certain attachments. If you read more than a few FDDs, you'll start to see much of the general legal language is similar. The FDD is communicating the franchise brand's history, facts, and other info that tells its unique "story." But not the whole story. I'll explain as we go.

The FTC and franchise attorneys are all very clear the FDD is not intended as a sales tool. I nod outwardly but beg to differ. While the FDD can't say, "We offer larger territories than our competitors," it will typically tell you how big the territories are. Nor can it say its royalties are better structured, or they have more reasonable late penalties, etc. They can't come out and say it, but you can put the pieces of the puzzle together. Jump over to the competitors' FDDs to see their territory size, their royalty schedule, their late payment fees, etc., and do your side-by-side comparisons. That's how FDDs can best be used by the informed prospect.

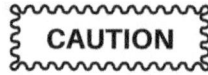

CAUTION

Just as we were coached in the military before taking an exam to RTFQ (read the fahking question), I'll caution you here to RTFFDD (read the fahking FDD).

Now, let's dive into the FDD to discern the story it's telling you.

Cover Page

Basic info about the offering. Initial Investment Range (the franchisor, based upon their experience, forecasts the range from lowest to highest for the Initial Investment). The dollar costs can vary a great deal based on a number of factors such as the size of the territory or territories you're securing, the equipment mix, vehicle(s) (purchased or leased), real estate considerations, buildouts, etc.

NOTE

Please keep in mind the word "initial" is too often overlooked or inadvertently conflated with "total." The FDD is written to illustrate your Initial Investment (typically the first three months of operations), not your Total Investment. I will discuss this difference and costs in more detail under ITEM 7 below.

The cover page also mentions two important points. First, you must have this document in your hands at least 14 days prior to you ever signing a franchise agreement. The FTC instituted this 14-day "cooling off period" about 45 years ago. Before that, some franchisors would bring you in for a Discovery Day (discussed later) where they performed their dog and pony show, got you all excited about their offering, and tried to get you to sign a very lengthy legal document without you having the time to review it. Since then, the FTC requires the FDD to be in your possession for at least 14 full days to give you time to review the document. This not only protects you from aggressive sales tactics, but it also throws cold water on a franchisee later experiencing buyer's remorse from claiming they were rushed into signing.

NOTE

Make good use of the 14 days—or longer. Take as much time as you need.

The cover page also mentions state regulations. There are 13 "registration states": California, Hawai'i, Illinois, Indiana, Maryland, Michigan, Minnesota, New York, North Dakota, Rhode Island, Virginia, Washington, and Wisconsin. Some of these states are fairly easy for the franchisor to register with, like Michigan and Wisconsin, where it's mostly a matter of filing a document and paying a fee, while others, such as California, Maryland, New York, Virginia, and Washington, have dedicated examiners who go over the document with a fine-tooth comb and will often require the franchisor to make some language changes to comply with their particular state's franchise regulations.

There are also franchise filing states where the franchisor must file a fairly simple notice with the state. These include Connecticut, Florida, Kentucky, Nebraska, North Carolina, South Carolina, South Dakota, Texas, and Utah. If the franchisor does not yet have a federally registered trademark, then they also need to file in Georgia and Louisiana.

All of the above is the franchisor's responsibility, not yours. If you are dealing with a fairly new brand and live in one of these states, just confirm they've done their homework.

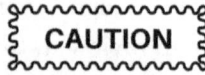

CAUTION

Do not interpret "registration" with any sort of "approval" or actual vetting of the franchisor. Registration simply means the document complies with that state's regulations.

You may also see a page titled "Special Risks to Consider About This Franchise." These are statements that arise from state regulators requiring certain declarations. Examples include, but are not limited to, "Out of State Dispute Resolution" (standard stuff—the franchisor wants the ability to resolve disputes in one state, not 50), "Spousal Liability" (pretty common to require the spouse to be included to preclude a rogue franchisee from trying to do a workaround for royalties and/or competition), "Short Operating History" (for newer brands), "Mandatory Minimum Payments" (standard clause—just make sure the minimums are reasonable!), "Financial Condition" (franchising is expensive and costs can place a newer franchisor in the red until the royalty stream and new franchise sales catch up or, perhaps, if the franchisor is in fact struggling).

Finally, there is one risk I've seen on an FDD that really caught my attention that I touched on earlier: *Turnover Rate*.

WARNING

This is a real-time warning from state regulators about relatively higher terminations and/or transfers within this brand compared to the industry norm. This deserves a great deal of your attention to understand what is happening in this brand—I cover this in more detail under my discussion on ITEM 20, later on.

On a related note, it takes a fairly extreme amount of fraud for the FTC to shut down a franchise system completely (again, search "Burger-IM"). The FTC will not alert you or protect you from buying into a bad idea or signing on with a bad actor. The FDD, in and of itself, with all the neat and orderly lawyerly language and charts, promotes an air of credibility. Don't confuse that with any sort of approval or brand competency.

I'm hoping by now you're in tune with the importance of differentiating the shit from the Shinola.

ITEM 1: THE FRANCHISOR AND ANY PARENTS, PREDECESSORS, OR AFFILIATES

The Franchisor

When multiple companies and umbrella companies are involved, this can get a little complicated and confusing. Be certain you know who controls what.

The Franchised Business (Sometimes Business Operations)

Pretty obvious—describes the business you will be operating and what makes it a franchise system.

Market and Competition

Most franchises are going to warn you there's competition (sometimes very stiff competition . . . hey, it's capitalism). That said, there are some industries that seem to be really oversaturated. Do lots of market research.

It's not just a matter to determine if there is room for one more. Is there also room for one more (yours) and other competitors who might follow? Can you capture market share and keep it?

Industry Specific Laws

Easily overlooked, this deserves some investigation on your part. Ask the franchisor about any laws that affect your future operation. Then, do some due diligence to be sure you have all the facts about licenses you might need (can you even qualify?). Be sure to get an attorney involved with subject matter expertise relative to the license involved. A good example would be working with an attorney who specializes in state liquor laws if you're opening a restaurant. Don't rely on the FDD to flag every law that might apply.

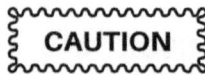

CAUTION

"Trust but verify" as President Ronald Reagan often said. BTW, Reagan was both enlisted and an officer in the Army Reserves.

ITEM 2: BUSINESS EXPERIENCE

Do the principals' experiences line up with what you're getting into? Is there a deep enough bench?

ITEM 3: LITIGATION

Unfortunately, we live in a litigious world. Seeing some litigation, particularly in very large brands, is not in and of itself a deal breaker. Within every franchise brand you'll see high and low performers. The bell curve is alive and well and living within most franchise brands. Low performers often look outward to find blame. Is the litigation from one disgruntled franchisee? Or is there a group of franchisees lining up against the franchisor? Are there similar claims being alleged? How many cases are there? Are they seeking damages? Injunctions? Is the franchisor just trying to enforce their non-compete clauses to protect the other owners and the brand?

Conversely, is the franchisor prone to suing franchisees they've terminated? Or is the lawsuit actually justified in protecting the brand from a rogue franchisee or group of franchisees?

Just like there are ambulance chasers in the personal injury world, there are lawyers who make a living pursuing the "deep pockets" of franchisors. If you see litigation, spend some time asking the franchisor for more background, reach out to the other party to hear their side of the story, and consult with your franchise attorney to get their take.

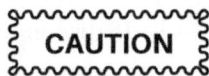

CAUTION

That said, if there's been some litigation and/or terminations that have concluded with NDAs (non-disclosure agreements) be on the alert for a franchisor trying to hide some dirty laundry. NDAs, in and of themselves, do not necessarily signal anything nefarious.

ITEM 4: BANKRUPTCY

This item requires a franchisor to disclose any bankruptcies by the franchisor, its parent company, affiliates, and/or individuals listed in

ITEM 2 for the past 10 years. One, two, or 20 bankruptcies beyond the 10-year limit need not be disclosed. Just like ITEM 3: LITIGATION, seeing something here bears a little more investigation. Get the franchisor's side of the story. Then, find ways to put your mind at ease or walk away.

ITEM 5: INITIAL FEE

Here's where you can feel your wallet start to get a little lighter just by reading it. In reality, spending money is just one small part of doing business.

Now, to that Initial Fee.

These are typically non-refundable. That said, if something goes sideways early on and the franchisor hasn't invested too much time or money up to this point, they might return a portion. Some states won't let the franchisor collect this fee until some degree of training and/or opening support is complete.

Franchise fees, in general, are on the rise. Everything has gotten more expensive in the franchise space: attorneys, marketing, broker commissions, technology platforms, etc.

Most franchisors won't negotiate their franchise fee with you. Early franchisors *might* be open to it. If discounts are offered they must be disclosed in the next FDD (which, in practice, serves as a deterrent for franchisors). Most do offer standard discounts if you buy additional territory or population size. As mentioned earlier, many franchisors offer discounts to veterans.

ITEM 6: FEES

Here's where some of the real money commitments are disclosed.

Royalty

Franchisors usually choose between two paths: a fixed, monthly/weekly fee or a percentage of sales. Make sure you understand exactly how the franchisor makes its money off of your operation. If it's a percentage, it's normally a percentage of the Gross Sales figure, not a percentage of the profits.

There are pros and cons to each method for both franchisee and franchisor.

A fixed monthly fee is a known quantity. That might be a pro for both parties. For the franchisor, it offers known cash flow for planning purposes. For the franchisee, fixed fees can be a real plus when you're crushing it. This method could lower your effective royalty percentage. On the downside, what if sales are slow? You're still on the hook for money that you might not be bringing in. For those in northern climates in a service-based business, you're still responsible to pay that monthly fee even though business is slow or paused. Also, the financial incentive to see your sales grow from the franchisor's perspective has evaporated. This is why I get a little uncomfortable on the fixed rate. With thousands of franchises out there, I don't wish to paint with too broad of a brush. It's just my experience that folks tend to not fully understand this metric.

As for percentage-based royalties, one could argue (and many do), the percentage-based scenario is fairer to both parties, as the franchisor makes very little when sales are slow and, conversely, when sales increase (in theory, thanks in large part to the franchisor), both parties are bringing in more money.

One con to this method is that at some point the franchisor may enjoy substantial benefits for little or no extra work on their end, particularly when compared to the efforts expended on lesser performing locations. That's just sort of the way this industry works, frankly. A small number of franchisors do offer scaled down royalties as sales increase to reward performance.

NOTE

All of the brands I work with have a scaled down royalty. I just sleep better at night doing it this way. It rewards top performers. I know our franchise partners certainly like it. I'd like to see this adopted more broadly in the franchise industry. It's the right thing to do.

Transfer Fee

Should you sell or otherwise transfer the rights to your franchise, the franchisor will charge you a fee. Some franchisors charge outrageous transfer fees (my opinion only). Yes, there will be resources expended by the franchisor, but the fee should be somewhere in the zone of reasonableness (this one's for you, John Malone). This fee might be negotiable if it's really out there. It goes without saying any negotiation you desire should take place before you sign, not after.

Renewal

Your Franchise Agreement is only for a fixed period of time. I've seen agreements anywhere from five to 15, even 20 years, with seven and 10 years being quite common. What happens when the term is up? Your franchise agreement should spell out the conditions you need to satisfy to renew.

NOTE

When you do renew, you'll be obligated to sign the then-current franchise agreement which will likely be different in some areas than the one you originally signed. A lot can change in five, seven, 10, or 15 years, and the franchisor is wise to make changes. You may have to expend significant sums to match the new requirements (brick and mortar franchises often demand upgrades), and you might see a different royalty scale, to give two examples. To put your mind at ease here, the franchisor is still trying to sell franchises and a competitive marketplace should inhibit overreach by the franchisor.

Marketing Fund, Local Ad Fund, Local Ad Co-ops

Expect to see where they want you spending your advertising monies. Some franchisors will spend on your behalf. Make sure you understand how much of your money is spent on your behalf. Really big name brands have very effective (and costly) national ad campaigns. You gotta pay to play in that sand box.

Tech Fees

Tech is becoming more and more complicated and costly, but absolutely necessary. Ask the company representative what their tech stack looks like. Also, ask existing franchisees how they like the tech and if it's adequate to manage and grow the business.

Training Costs

Most franchisors include training in the franchise fee. However, I've seen a recent uptick in franchisors charging a separate training fee. I believe this is a back door way to pad the franchise fee and would like to see this practice halted.

You may also incur some additional costs if you bring more than the allotted number of staff to training. This item should also identify what corporate will charge you if additional training is needed later on.

Noncompliance

Hammer Time!

The franchisor needs a hammer to keep the system running without distractions. Late reports trigger late payments, which trigger extra work for the staff. Poor customer service from a sloppy franchisee needs fixing. Stat!

The franchise agreement has mechanisms to protect the brand and, ultimately, your investment as well. Is the hammer of sufficient size without going overboard? Probably a discussion item with your franchise attorney as he should know some comparisons.

Brand Development

You may or may not see this item in your FDD. If it's there, ask the representative to share how they're spending that money. Those funds are meant for improving and promoting the brand and growing *your* sales, *not* for new franchise recruitment.

ITEM 7: INITIAL INVESTMENT

Here, you'll find things like your franchise fee and other amounts initially payable to the franchisor, extra territory fees (if any), construction and leasehold improvements, lease deposits, equipment costs, initial inventory, computers, phones, grand opening costs, marketing, uniforms, insurance, travel, professional fees (attorney, CPA), vehicle costs, vehicle wraps, first few months of wages, and operating cash on hand.

You'll see a range of costs from low to high. Some of these you may have influence over or you may be well positioned with your own resources. Example: You already own a laptop and cell phone; congrats, you just saved $2,000. If you already possess a suitable pickup truck that merely needs to be wrapped, you probably just reduced the high end of that initial investment estimate by at least $40,000.

Not unlike building a house, do expect some cost overruns. Many businesses fail early on due to cash flow issues. Be sure you have sufficient cash backup planned. Look closely at ITEM 7 with your accountant!

NOTE

Remember, the costs listed in ITEM 7 are typically only the initial investment for the first three months. Your total investment will be higher.

ITEM 8: RESTRICTIONS ON SOURCES OF PRODUCTS AND SERVICES

My one comment here is to make sure you aren't forced to buy basic commodities like toilet paper, paper towels, unmarked straws, etc., through the franchisor or its affiliates. Some franchisors, particularly in the food space, have been called out on this practice. Conduct a search on "reasons for Quiznos® failures." Also, if the franchisor receives rebates from vendors, what is done with the rebate monies?

ITEM 9: FRANCHISEE'S OBLIGATIONS

This is merely a handy index you can reference to help locate contract language in the franchise agreement about your various obligations.

ITEM 10: FINANCING

A few franchisors might offer in-house financing of some or all of the franchise fee. They may also fund certain other expenses you incur. If that is the case, you're essentially taking out a loan with them instead of the bank.

Anecdotally, most franchisors do not offer in-house financing. If they do offer financing, that would make it easier for funding the rest of your initial investment. I cover the more popular forms of financing in more detail in CHAPTER 10: Financing.

ITEM 11: FRANCHISOR'S ASSISTANCE, ADVERTISING, COMPUTER SYSTEMS, AND TRAINING

This tells you exactly what you're getting from the franchisor in terms of initial and ongoing support. It should also give details about where training is held, by whom, the topics covered, and the length of training.

ITEM 12: TERRITORY

This is a super important item that needs a closer look by your franchise attorney.

WARNING

Do not skim this item lightly, nor assume you know what it's saying. There is some very specific "franchise-ese" that can trip you up. Look closely at the size of your territory in terms of geography and population, how many other territories can be awarded next to yours (for certain brands, the more the merrier in some ways, but it's a matter of degrees), and what restrictions you have on servicing outside your territory.

Some service brands will let you perform work outside your area, but not let you market there (as long as it's not in someone else's territory), while others are very strict.

Ask your broker/company rep to compare with other competing brands: Why is your single territory comprised of 350,000 population, while Brand X offers 750,000? If so, what's the justification? There may well be one.

Doubtful, but ask!

The Territory Game

Franchisors make money two ways: franchise fees and royalties. One way to boost the franchise fee revenue piece is to offer multiple "territories," particularly in the service space. Territories are also sometimes referred to as "units" or "locations."

Philosophically, I believe a single territory should be of sufficient size to support a franchise business. I mean, that just makes sense, right?

Within the parking lot striping industry, I have competitors selling territories with as few as 350,000 in population. 350,000 is simply not big enough (in my humble view gained from 14 years in the business). So, they encourage the buyers to acquire more territories, which means more money out of your pocket and into theirs. We charge $50,000 for our largest territory (~3.75 million population) while three of my competitors charge anywhere from $250,000 to $350,000 for that same size. This also reinforces my suggestion to look at competitor FDDs.

I'm aware of another brand in a different industry that requires a minimum of two territories to be purchased. Well, why not just make the single territory size larger in the first place? Because they then can't play "the territory game" and collect additional fees up front or announce, "Two (three, four, five) new locations awarded!"

Part of generating interest in a franchise brand is the pace with which they're selling franchises and the ability to cast the subliminal FOMO (fear of missing out) message around. When you buy one of our brands we simply announce, "New franchise awarded!" The territory size doesn't matter in our PR efforts. On the other hand, my competition would announce, "Five new territories (locations/units/franchises) awarded!" under the exact same circumstances.

If it were up to me, this practice would be prohibited. Unfortunately, it's now ingrained in the franchise ecosystem. I'd really like to see this practice called out by the Responsible Franchising crowd.

Look, just take "the territory game" for what it is in your deliberations.

ITEM 13: TRADEMARKS

As I mentioned earlier, there are three elements to a franchise relationship, one of them being a trademark.

This item alerts you to the trademarks the franchisor either possesses or licenses from a third party. They will be identified as follows:

Principal Trademarks Registered With the United States Patent and Trademark Office

The trademark(s) will likely include word marks and logo(s). Some trademarks might be "in progress" at the U.S. Patent and Trademark Office (USPTO). They will be identified as follows: Principal trademarks not registered with the United States Patent and Trademark Office.

This means the franchisor has filed for the trademark and they are awaiting a final decision by the USPTO. Conscientious franchisors will have consulted a competent trademark attorney to see if they think their word mark or logo should pass muster with the USPTO. There's always a chance that a USPTO examiner finds a reason to reject an application for a trademark. In this case, the franchisor may attempt to challenge or negotiate with another party holding a similar word mark or logo to allow use.

It's generally up to the franchisor to defend its trademarks should anyone else use them inappropriately or confusingly. Trademark law is a highly specialized legal area of expertise in and of itself. If you have trademark concerns, I suggest you hire an attorney who specializes in trademarks.

ITEM 14: PATENTS, COPYRIGHTS, AND PROPRIETARY INFORMATION

This item covers intellectual property the franchisor wishes to protect. This is for your benefit as much as the franchisor's. Without the "secret sauce," what do you have, exactly?

Guard the franchisor's intellectual property as if it were your own.

ITEM 15: OBLIGATION TO PARTICIPATE IN THE ACTUAL OPERATION OF THE FRANCHISE BUSINESS

There really aren't very many true "passive ownership" franchises out there. Businesses take work. New businesses are like newborn babies.

You need to do everything for them. If that's not your idea of fun, then you need to hire someone to do it for you.

ITEM 15 protects the franchisor (and the rest of the franchisees) from someone buying a franchise and then not working it. Depending upon the type of business, absent or part-time owners can cause great harm to other owners (think of the service industry and unanswered phone calls or a mishandled national account).

If you can't meet the obligations of ITEM 15 yourself or with a rock star manager, do both you and the franchisor a big favor and don't sign the franchise agreement.

ITEM 16: RESTRICTIONS ON WHAT THE FRANCHISEE MAY SELL

If you haven't seen the movie *The Founder*, please find a way to see it. And, if it's been a while since you last saw it, see it again! This is my favorite business movie, as it gives us a window into how franchising really took shape through the vision of Ray Kroc, played by Michael Keaton.

Michael Keaton as Ray Kroc in The Founder

While the concept of franchising had been around for years prior, Kroc really invented the modern day version of what franchising is today.

The McDonald brothers focused on systems and processes. Kroc then took that to a new level at scale.

In one scene, Kroc discovers one of his franchisees is selling chicken sandwiches, corn on the cob, putting lettuce and tomatoes on the burgers, and having three pickles instead of two.

Kroc flips out.

The moral of the story is simple, but incredibly important: Follow the franchisor's system religiously. If you're a franchisee in the dryer vent cleaning industry, don't start offering window installations. If you run a quick service restaurant, don't get cute with the menu without clearing it first with the franchisor.

In sum, follow the system.

ITEM 17: RENEWAL, TERMINATION, TRANSFER, AND DISPUTE RESOLUTION

ITEM 17 is a handy cross reference table to help you easily locate certain pieces of information in the franchise agreement. The franchise agreement will go into great detail regarding renewals, terminations, transfers, and dispute resolution, and this table provides summarized language on each topic.

This is also the place you'll find the length of the term for the franchise agreement.

Term Length

A few words about term length. Most franchisors have some logic to their term lengths. Most. Since the brands I work with are in the service space, I think seven years makes the most sense for our sector. I read somewhere that a good number of business owners wish to make a big change (expand or sell) somewhere around the seven year mark. Ever hear of the "seven year itch"?

Five years seems too short to me, and anything over 10 years seems a bit too long for a service brand. But it's not out of the norm.

Big investment franchises will sometimes have 15 to 20 year terms. An investor will want to see longevity baked in if they're plopping down millions to open a restaurant.

Be wary of franchises that lock you in for an unreasonable term. None of us has a crystal ball.

ITEM 18: PUBLIC FIGURES

This is pretty self-explanatory. In a hypersensitive social media environment, my only concern here would be if the franchisor has aligned with a celebrity who is controversial or later causes problems. Politics are the third rail these days.

NOTE

My editor says I shouldn't mention the Jared from Subway® debacle, so I won't.

ITEM 19: FINANCIAL PERFORMANCE REPRESENTATIONS

Everyone buying into a franchise wants to make money, right? Here's where you can find out (to a certain degree) what kind of money might be made.

Sort of.

I say "sort of" because there are sometimes weaknesses and/or gaps in the way franchisors present their numbers. For example, if the franchisor chooses, they can simply post Gross Sales figures for their franchise locations. Gross Sales is one KPI, but it doesn't tell you if the franchisees are profitable.

Some franchisors will post information that's only volunteered by their franchisees. Expect lots of folks to be reluctant to send their numbers out into the ether.

Some franchisors do not make any financial representations. Most brands have top performers in weaker markets and weaker performers in premium markets, and everything in between. Franchisee success rates are very much individually driven.

I highly encourage all prospects to contact current and past owners to get the unvarnished truth and discuss their experience with the brand to make an informed decision.

Who better to tell you the whole story than the owners who are living the brand? Don't stop your research simply because you might be seeing some great numbers in ITEM 19.

Past performance does not necessarily predict future performance. Is the market shifting downward? ITEM 19 can't tell the whole story.

As I mentioned earlier, if the franchisor chooses to not make earnings claims, then no one involved with the potential sale of that franchise from corporate may make any sort of claim, including winks and nods. If you're using a broker, they must not be making any financial claims either. If you're getting "off the record" type info from sales, be very careful. That's out of bounds. Big red flag.

In the middle of writing this section I received a request to connect with someone on LinkedIn in a related franchise space. I agreed and he convinced me to jump on a call. Despite telling him I was a very unlikely franchise candidate (as in no chance at all), he proceeded to pitch me as a franchise prospect and violate the no earnings claims rule with outrageous profit claims using wildly unrealistic margins. I was dumbfounded. Then, to top it all off, he sent me an AI-generated summary of the call putting in print his blatant violations. Unbelievable! This little exercise solidified my suspicions there's a lot of bending of the rules out there.

Back to how you approach earnings claims and forecasts for yourself. Franchisees, unlike brokers working without an ITEM 19, are free to share any information they wish and, again, are your very best source of information when performing due diligence.

Have I mentioned the need to talk to lots of franchisees, past and present, enough yet?

Be certain you have a financial expert take a look at any earnings claims in ITEM 19 as well as having them take a look at the franchisor's financials (discussed below in ITEM 21).

While ITEM 19 focuses on money, money doesn't tell the whole story. Be sure you're looking at the whole picture, not just ITEM 19.

Earnings Claims Nuances

Here's a really nuanced wrinkle that even slips by seasoned franchise professionals. I have seen brand new franchisors use their own company store financials to create their ITEM 19 (the business they are modeling the franchise after).

There are several problems with that. First, it's awesome that they're doing $2 million (pick a number), but it might have taken them 10 to 15 years to get to these numbers and there is a lot of repeat and referral business baked into those figures. Plus, they most likely didn't have the same territory constraints you now face. Those numbers can unintentionally deceive the prospective franchisee.

Is that legal? Ask a lawyer.

Are they in technical compliance with the FTC's FDD rules? Depends on how it's worded.

Do those numbers run the risk of setting false expectations for the new franchisee? Probably.

On purpose???

Franchisees buy into a system so they can fast-track their growth. They don't want to take 10 to 15 years to get to $2 million. When dealing with a very fresh concept, make sure you understand how they achieved those numbers, how long it took them to get there, and what's their plan to get *you* to those numbers in what amount of time.

An Interesting ITEM 19

Finally, doing research for this manual, I stumbled upon a survival franchise concept founded by a retired Army Colonel. Its ITEM 19 states: *Please do not ask us for any help estimating your financial results as a franchisee. We would like to help you, but cannot due to the high risk of lawsuits due to horrible regulations and our legal system.*

A novel approach for sure.

In a recent article in *Franchise Times*, the good Colonel also laments the struggles his potential franchisees face in getting financing. The *Times* surmises: *Banks don't like to fund concepts that are based upon the collapse of society.*

You can't make this stuff up.

Up next, one of the most important items in the FDD.

ITEM 20: OUTLETS AND FRANCHISEE INFORMATION

ITEM 20 has lots of tables!

At first glance, it's a bit overwhelming. ITEM 20 is really trying to tell you the story of the brand; where it's been, where it is, where it thinks it's going, and its trend lines. ***It can also be the most important item you review if there are underlying problems in the brand.***

First, let's discuss Transfers. I touched on them earlier.

Transfer: the assignment of your franchise agreement to another entity. Transfers are pretty common in the course of business. They can be both normal (positive or somewhat benign in nature) or they may be signaling a deeper problem.

Folks may need/want to sell their franchises for any number of reasons. Ideally, they sell to make a profit. Other reasons include life-style changes, medical reasons, other interests, or the business is struggling.

Transfers in and of themselves are not a bad thing. But they could be the canary in the coal mine, too, if folks are bailing out with pennies on the dollar. Ask questions about any transfers you see.

Non-renewals: this might be an indicator of a problem in the system. If you're seeing a number of franchises coming up for renewal accompanied by a large percentage of non-renewals, this may be telling you there's a problem that's been percolating. Ask questions.

Re-acquired by Franchisor: this could be a sign of some trouble, or it can be a very healthy signal where the franchisor takes back a struggling franchise and operates that location. Here, the franchisor still believes in its brand and goes through the trouble to re-acquire that location.

Signed but Not Opened: there are often new darlings in the franchise industry, frequently in the food or wellness spaces. These hit the market and it's almost like the real estate bidding wars during COVID, folks are flocking to these new brands. This is mostly driven by the FSOs, broker networks, and hype.

Be careful of brands with lots of new signings with a huge lag in openings. Brick and mortar stores do take a long time to open, so this lag might be very normal. But, just to be sure, reach out to those who've signed and ask them how things are going and what's causing the delays. Watch for excessive "Signed but Not Opened" numbers.

Termination: simply means the franchise was removed from the system. I don't like this term because it doesn't tell the whole story.

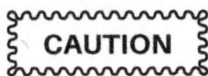

CAUTION

FDDs are issued annually, typically in March and April; meaning the information can become stale as time passes until the next FDD. If a brand is suddenly experiencing a spike in terminations since their latest FDD release, they are under no obligation to disclose this until the next FDD (unless you ask). Therefore, you should ask the franchisor (the broker may not know these details) to bring you up to speed on any new terminations since the last FDD was issued. If there are terminations, have them explain the reasons behind them (then verify later with these former franchisees for their side of the story). And, get it in writing (email should suffice).

In military terms, a termination is a bit like a discharge. A franchisee who had a medical condition or injury that prevented them from operating the business might ask to be terminated (think honorable/medical discharge). In this scenario they might also be listed under Ceased Operations for Other Reasons (there might be some very slight variances in the way these are listed from one FDD to the next).

A franchisor who discovers a new franchisee that is not a good cultural fit might try to unwind the franchise agreement soon after signing and part ways amicably. One might consider this a general discharge under honorable conditions. I wouldn't hold this against the franchisor, per se. They are simply trying to protect the brand and avoid deeper problems later. That's the sign of a mature franchisor. As I mentioned earlier, perhaps their vetting process is worthy of some honest critique.

Or you've got a rogue franchisee who forms a side LLC to siphon off work and avoid royalties. That's stealing. They would need to be terminated and you might call this a dishonorable discharge. You can't have dishonest people in your system. This is not the franchisor's fault.

Another scenario has a franchisee simply failing while many others are doing fine. They've done their best, but they're just not making it. Perhaps they aren't cut out for business. Maybe there are very difficult local market conditions that other franchisees aren't experiencing. They're running out of money, and they need out. This one's a bit tricky for the franchisor to navigate. Their overall system is mostly working well, but this particular franchisee is struggling. Most franchise agreements have a clause that places the franchisee on the hook for the remainder of the term of the franchise agreement for some minimum royalties and other fees due.

Does the franchisor chase them for money they don't have? Do they drag them to court or arbitration? I hope not. That would be Irresponsible Franchising. I suppose I'd call this another general discharge under honorable conditions.

Finally, you've got a large percentage of the franchise brand that is struggling, and the system doesn't really work at the level it should. While not all locations are failing (some may even be thriving), there are lots of struggles across the brand and franchises are closing/transferring at a very high rate. What's a "high rate"? I looked around and can find no accepted metric, though I've been told the Small Business Administration won't touch a loan for a brand with a 40% turnover rate.

Personally, I'd be very concerned long before I saw a 40% turnover or termination rate.

Just because they're still signing new franchisees (LinkedIn is full of these types of announcements) doesn't mean everything is hunky dory.

Thank You Drill Sergeant, May I Have Another?

Is ITEM 20 being overlooked by franchise prospects? It must be, because I'm aware of countless brands with high failure rates that are still selling franchises.

One service brand in particular comes to mind; it has a very high termination rate and sells to veterans and veteran family members. In my opinion, they should stop selling franchises and make their singular focus the success of existing owners, not introducing new owners into a system hoping it might work out better for them than others.

My heart breaks when I see the picture of the new veteran franchisee smiling and excited for their next chapter, apparently oblivious to the high failure rate of the brand and the increased likelihood of their own future struggles. The worst part? It's run by a fellow veteran.

They also have a 15-year term for no apparent business-case justification (at least from the franchisee's perspective, in my opinion), which can handcuff the franchisee for a very extended time.

Some of their franchisees appear to be doing quite well. But, the failure rate is way out of whack. I wish them no ill will. This brand must survive and then thrive for its existing franchisees. The alternative is unacceptable.

Confession Time. The scenario above was the original impetus for this book. Everything I've written prior to this chapter and after this chapter was designed to get to this point in the manual. This is my biggest axe to grind. If I can save one veteran from making a bad choice, I will consider this book a success.

Whew! Grinding of Axe Complete

I'm hoping my discussion here will help folks understand that ITEM 20 deserves a very close look and the language used by the FTC does not tell the whole story.

WARNING

Ignoring ITEM 20 can be disastrous.

ITEM 21: FINANCIAL STATEMENTS

You're going to need a CPA to help you with this (or a seasoned franchise attorney) so you can understand what the franchisor's financial statements are telling you.

Big name, long-established brands should show some pretty good numbers. That goes without saying. Newer brands will have much smaller numbers, naturally, and some state regulators may even issue a warning about limited capital. That's not unusual.

Recent IRS rulings changed the way some items are accounted for and can make the numbers look worse than they really are for franchisors. Talk to a knowledgeable CPA if you want a better understanding.

ITEM 22: CONTRACTS

When you join a franchise brand, you'll likely be signing other contracts as well. ITEM 22 of the FDD covers things like a sample of the Franchise Agreement you'll sign, State Specific Addenda, Exhibits to the Franchise Agreement, Operating Territory Acknowledgement, Statement of Franchisee's Owners Exhibits, Franchise Owner and Spousal Agreement and Guaranty, Assignment of Telephone Numbers and Digital Media, ACH Authorization, General Release, and others.

The phone number you use for the business must belong to the franchisor (or at least they need a mechanism in place to recover it should something change) and the social media channels also belong to the franchisor. Don't take it personally.

ITEM 23: RECEIPTS

Early on I mentioned the "cooling off period" of 14 days from the time you receive the FDD until you may sign a franchise agreement. This item helps document that 14 day cooling off.

Most (I hope all) franchisors will use some sort of electronic means to document your "receipt" of the FDD (think DocuSign® or similar).

Signing the receipt does not obligate you to anything whatsoever. It's merely your acknowledgement that you received the FDD, not that you've read it.

NOTE

Please be respectful of the broker's time and efforts and promptly sign the ITEM 23 Receipt unless you are certain you have no interest at all in the franchise. In that case, please alert them to your decision so they can move on. It's the polite and proper thing to do.

If you find yourself really interested in pursuing the franchise, please make good use of these 14 days (or as long as you need) to complete your due diligence and consult with subject matter experts like your franchise attorney, CPA, industry expert, etc.

Also, don't be pressured into thinking you need to make a decision once the 14 days are up. That's a tacky approach to sales.

Whew! That's a lot to digest.

Now, let's look at some franchise opportunities out there.

This gets pretty wild!

CHAPTER 8

FINDING THE PERFECT FRANCHISE

The perfect franchise is revealed on the next page.

THIS PAGE INTENTIONALLY LEFT BLANK

There's no such thing as the perfect franchise.

CHAPTER 9

FINDING THE RIGHT FRANCHISE FOR YOU

Reality check. The perfect franchise does not exist. No franchise system is without its flaws and imperfections, including ours. As you approach the choice of which franchise system to join, you shouldn't let perfect be the enemy of the good.

In the next chapter, we will discuss finding the right franchise for *you*.

You may have noticed I've been using the number "almost 4,000 active franchises" throughout this manual. According to Edith Wiseman, President of FranDATA, the leading data collector for the industry, the actual count for 2023 was 3,937 active franchises (countless inactive) with 450 being brand new franchise concepts.[1] The industry is pumping out more than one new franchise concept per day. They run the gamut from the common to the obscure.

If money is your sole motivator, then you're able to be dispassionate about your choices. Run some comparisons on a number of brands that fit your budget and bring you the best chance for the bigger ROI based upon the ITEM 19s. That's a much easier exercise than finding a brand you can be passionate about.

Personally, I need something to be passionate about over and above just the money piece. I'd also want a franchisor who shares my core values, a product or service I can get excited about, and something that's competitive where my own efforts can affect sales and winning. But that's me. You need to figure out your own motivators and your own *why*.

Riches in Niches

This is the world in which I see the most exciting and interesting opportunities—the niches.

Find products or services that are underserved or under the radar.

You might find gold.

"Hot" Franchises Can Sometimes Burn

Over the years there have been many "hot" franchise brands or concepts that have crashed and burned.

Frozen yogurt (froyo) was the place to be not that many years ago. Some brands and owners did very well and continue to do very well. Many others have closed their doors. TCBY® once had 3,000 locations in the 1990s. They now list approximately 250 on their website.

The fancy cookie and cupcake sectors are all the rage at the moment. Where do they go from here? Are they the next froyo? I don't know. Some are saying these hot brands can't keep pace with the early returns they achieved and are beginning to crumble. Others say they have a long run still ahead of them. I have no crystal ball.

iSoldit® on eBay® had 100 locations within 18 months of launch in 2002 and are now down to about 10 locations. The July 12, 2004, issue of *Entrepreneur Magazine* featured eBay drop off stores as "What's Hot."[1]

Curves® Fitness for Women had over 10,000 locations worldwide in 2006. Now? Roughly 200.[2]

Quiznos was on fire in the early 2000s and had about 4,700 units at its peak in 2007. Fewer than 200 remain today.[3]

Boring suits me just fine. On the other hand, I've also missed out on some great opportunities over the years I assumed wouldn't last. Hindsight being 20/20 and all.

Definitely be certain whatever you're looking at buying into can't be "Amazon'd" or that one more small leap in technology will make your concept obsolete (EV vehicles don't need mufflers, the cameras at iSoldit were replaced by smart phones), or you are chronically at risk due to a single point of failure scenario. As one example, I've read of franchise failures in the martial arts space. Buyers are told they need not have any martial arts experience because they can hire that talent. If there is no one to say "Bow to your sensei" to the kids, you're done.

If you're jumping on a bandwagon, make sure it's got wheels built for the long haul.

Beware the Hype

Now would be a good time to forewarn you about some of the hype you'll see. I have to chuckle when I see certain brands saying things like "Get your share of the $20 gazillion billion home services industry!" That's great, but how big is your slice of that industry?

"Recession resistant" is very common. I'll confess I've used that term because it actually fits. It's probably one of the most over-used terms in the industry, which can diminish its real value and meaning.

The other franchise sales phrase used almost universally is "Be in business for yourself, not by yourself." That's franchising in a nutshell—if it's done right.

"Elite profits." This one takes the cake. What does that even mean?

Have a little fun with this and play Franchise Cliché Bingo as you conduct your research.

Types of Franchise Concepts

The following is but a small sampling of the types of franchises out there. It's by no means comprehensive.

Automotive: Accessories, bed liners, dealerships, detailing, fleet washing, repairs, rust-proofing. Cars are still big business.

B2B: Accounting, asphalt maintenance/markings, consulting, copy and print shops, dental equipment repair, dumpster rentals, dumpster compaction, ink cartridge refilling, insurance, lab testing, payroll, restoration, staffing, temporary wall systems, vehicle wraps, web design, etc. Some very large customers can be found in this space.

Elder Care: Boomers are aging and business is booming (pun intended). Lots of franchise brands in this space.

Faith-Based: Mix of food, service, and other businesses.

Food/Drinks: Huge category! Brew pubs, chicken and chicken wings, coffee, cookies, cupcakes, food trucks, juice bars, pizza, quick service restaurants (aka QSR), salads, smoothies, specialty foods, sub shops, yogurt, the list goes on.

Health and Beauty: Very big part of the franchise world. Think barbershops, body sculpting, fitness, gyms, lashes, massages, nails, styling salons, waxing, etc. Most of these use the subscription model, making them very popular. You generally don't need a very large territory for these to work.

Home Services: Carpet cleaning, electrical, epoxy floors, furniture repair, grout repair, gutters, holiday and landscape lighting, home cleaning, junk removal, kitchen and bath remodeling, lawn care, painting, plumbing, pressure washing, renovations, tree removal, etc.

Hotels: Serious money investments.

Kid Stuff: Kid care, kid gaming, kid gyms, kid learning, kid music, kid sports, kid swimming, etc.

Mosquito Killing: Mosquito killing really falls under the Home Services category above. It's such an interesting segment, I thought I'd give it its own category.

Not that many years ago the mosquito killing franchise concept was looked upon as novel or strange. For an awfully small insect, it sure commands a lot of love from the franchise industry. Mosquito killing is big business!

Alphabetically, you've got MissQuito®, Mosquito Authority®, Mosquito Hunter®, Mosquito Joe®, Mosquito Magician®, Mosquito Marshall®, Mosquito Mary's®, Mosquito Mike®, Mosquito Nix®, Mosquito One®, Mosquito Sheriff®, Mosquito Shield®, Mosquito Squad®, and likely some others I may be overlooking or are soon to launch. Certain other franchise brands in the lawn care space also offer mosquito services as an additional service. Look out mosquitoes. The franchise world is coming after you! This is a subscription model that makes it a popular space for franchising.

Pets: Pet related franchises have exploded in recent years. Pet care, pet hotels, pet memorials, pet sitting/walking, pet waste removal (I count no fewer than 10 franchise brands scooping poop), the list goes on in this space with multiple brands within each particular pet sector. Many of these use the subscription model.

Sports/Fitness: Boxing, golf, gyms, martial arts, Pilates, trampoline parks, water slides, yoga, etc.

Unusual and Unique: Anger rooms, bed bug killing, Canada goose-chasing dogs (my favorite unusual concept simply because it makes me smile, not commenting on its viability), cannabis, charcuterie boards, crime scene cleanup, dating, deer repelling, drones, escape rooms, float therapy, goat rental (yes, you read that right), lice removal, mold-sniffing dogs, oxygen bars, pet cremation (for when your mold-sniffing or Canada goose-chasing dog passes away), pub cycles, sign spinning (attention-getters standing on street corners spinning signs for local businesses), survivalist, vaping, virtual reality, wildlife containment, and who knows how many others are floating around out there. A few of these look to be very viable businesses. A number of these have sputtered out. Some seem . . . well, do your own diligence. And then some.

Franchise Resales

There's one more category I wish to bring to your attention and that is franchise resales. The name speaks for itself, but there's a little more to it.

These are existing franchises from across the franchise spectrum. The owners are looking to sell for any number of reasons.

If it's a successful business and the franchisees now want to cash out, these businesses will come at a premium. What's a fair price? Consult with a CPA or broker who's dealt with transactions like this. You might see 3X of EBITDA (earnings before interest, taxes, depreciation and amortization) at the low end and maybe 5X to 7X (or even more) at the high end. Lots of factors go into assessing the value with the type of business sector likely being the biggest determinant. Remember, everything is negotiable, and these situations often provide owner financing for a portion of the deal.

At the other end of the spectrum you might find a franchisee who is struggling and simply needs out. Maybe some major life event has occurred (medical condition, needs to move, etc.). You can likely snag the business for pennies on the dollar. Be certain you know why it's struggling. Is the cause of the struggle due to the owner not being focused on the business and distracted by other things? Or is the concept a complete dud to begin with? Another shit from Shinola moment.

One of our former franchise owners was distracted by a full time position elsewhere along with another situation taking up all his time. He was near last in sales in 2020. We found a buyer who mostly made him whole (which is rare when a business is struggling). The seller held paper for the buyer and two years later that location had soared to number one in sales and the loan was repaid early. The system works if you work the system. That business is now worth far more than what it cost to purchase.

Those deals are out there, but they are a little tricky to find. Also, there might be a great deal like the one I describe above, but it's in another state. That won't do you much good.

Check BizBuySell.com for listings and discuss with a franchise broker.

One last suggestion on resales: If you've found a brand you really like, but they are sold out in your area, it never hurts to pick up the phone and call the owner. They might be open to selling but haven't taken the steps to begin that process.

Which To Choose?

Maybe something sparked your interest or caught your eye in the list above. There are likely any number of franchises in the categories above that can turn out to be the right franchise for you. Start performing some internet sleuthing. Fill out the online forms all franchisor websites offer to gather info. If you are working with a broker, be sure to tell them what piques your interest.

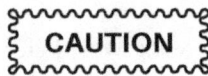

CAUTION

For those of us with undiagnosed ADD (like me) we can sometimes be like the dog that gets distracted by the squirrel. Squirrel, in this case, meaning a franchise that grabs your attention for the wrong reasons and distracts you from the task at hand (finding a solid franchise opportunity that's right for you). You might chase that squirrel only to discover that it's a rat. Remember, a squirrel is nothing more than a rat with better PR.

Gathering Franchise Intel

If you aren't already working with a broker, once you start filling out those online forms requesting info you'll likely be dropped into a CRM program that will help trigger an email/text campaign telling you bits of information about the brand. The CRM program will also help the broker keep track of you, your level of interest, pertinent notes from calls you have, emails, texts, etc.

Once you feel you're starting to register as a five on a scale of one to 10 in terms of interest, it might be time to schedule a call with the sales rep to hear their pitch and ask for the FDD, if it hasn't already been sent. Often, you'll have to fill out an application before you can receive the FDD.

Conscientious franchisors will use a background check service if you start to get really interested. Don't take it personally.

Once you have that FDD, use my suggestions from CHAPTER 6 to go over it.

Discovery Day (Sometimes Called Decision Day)

If you're really interested in a particular brand and they're interested in you, you will likely be invited to a Discovery Day visit—most often at your own expense. Some franchisors will offer to reimburse you for those travel expenses if you sign on.

Here's where you'll either visit world headquarters, meet at a franchisee's location with corporate staff, or connect via an online video call, so they may put their best foot forward in a presentation, aka the dog and pony show.

If you haven't already, try to visit with one or two franchisees without corporate present to get the unfiltered truth about a day in the life either before or after Discovery Day.

Some brands have started calling these visits *Decision Days*. It's a pretty effective psychological tool to move folks closer to a decision.

Do not fall into the trap of thinking you have to decide then and there or even right after your visit.

Once you've found a brand or some brands you are serious about, you have to prepare to finance your franchise. This next chapter takes a very deep dive into financing.

Chapter 10

Financing

Overview

If you've made it this far, needing funding—congratulations! You have successfully completed vetting yourself and the franchise you hope to join, or you are closing in on that decision.

Now, all you have to do is pay for it.

Easier said than done.

But absolutely doable for most.

Funding is one of those bogeymen that people assume is outside of their reach, which prevents many from ever investigating the possibilities of business ownership. It is always worth exploring your options before making a decision based on your risk tolerance, the organization you are buying into, your business goals (and family goals), and your confidence in your ability to meet the challenges of owning a business.

The first thing you must do is take stock of your financial situation. You need to create a personal financial statement for yourself and anyone going into business with you. This will give you a clear understanding of your assets and vulnerabilities. Once you have those statements in hand and have a strong understanding of your assets and what you can risk, then it is time to forge a plan for acquiring and operating your franchise.

Your Personal Credit Score Matters

For lending, your personal credit score most likely will play a big role in getting funding. If you don't have ideal credit make a plan to get your credit back on track and stick to it. There are free resources out there to help. The VA's Veterans Benefits Banking Program (VBBP 2.0) might be a good place to start. Visit VeteransBenefitsBanking.org for more info. What's the minimum score you should shoot for to obtain a loan? My friends in the SBA banking world say 680-700, though they have seen traditional lending below that score occasionally.

Self-Funding Sources

Family and Friends Lending

From my experience, some franchisees rely on family to fund their purchases, a sort of familial angel investor. Should you go this route, make sure you put it all in writing. It protects both of you down the line, regardless of whether the investment pays off or not. Should the business fail, what will be the damage to the family relationships?

Retirement Plan Funding

There are strict rules surrounding IRA, Thrift Savings Plans (TSP), and 401(k) funds as funding sources. If you completed your personal financial statement as recommended above, you will need to determine the terms and conditions of using retirement funds to finance your franchise. There are penalties for early withdrawal and other concerns. Some plans allow short-term loans where you pay yourself interest on the loan. I once used my 401(k) in that manner. Each plan is different. Consult with a tax professional.

ROBS Program

Another way to use retirement funds is what is called the Rollover as Business Startup Program (ROBS). Essentially you are creating a C-Corp to invest in yourself from funds in your 401(k), IRA, or TSP. ROBS have lots of IRS and tax implications and should not be undertaken lightly. Certain third-party vendors specialize in helping you get through the necessary paperwork for both an up-front and ongoing management fee. One big advantage is the absence of a minimum monthly payment which is particularly helpful for start-ups. Another advantage to the ROBS Program is that your credit score doesn't matter since it's your money. This is commonly used as the equity piece in SBA financing.

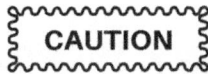

CAUTION

I've seen ROBS used, but it does make me a bit nervous. I think it boils down to a matter of degrees. Are you tapping into 10% to 20% of your life savings or 90%? How old are you? What's your time horizon to make up for any possible losses? Do not pursue this means of funding without thoroughly discussing this with a qualified CPA/tax advisor and franchise attorney.

Home Equity Line of Credit (HELOC)

HELOC loans are fairly easy to obtain if you've got equity in your home. Once the line of credit is established the bank won't care if you're buying a new car, adding a swimming pool, funding a franchise, or spending it on boats and Harleys. Generally speaking, it's yours to do with as you please. Many HELOCs allow interest only payments with a balloon payment at the end of the term (often 10 years). This can be a real plus in helping you control costs and cash flow early on while the business gets off the ground. Even if you don't use the

HELOC and fund a different way, it's nice to have some emergency fund access should the need arise. Discuss this with your local banker.

Leasing

Most franchises have equipment requirements. Rather than depleting cash reserves on equipment, it may prove to be a better idea to lease your equipment to save any cash reserves for your start-up and growth plans. Depending on the requirements from the franchisor and the number of vendors available to you, rates and terms are going to vary. Make sure you treat any lease agreement the way you would buying a car or a home: Do your homework, have questions ready, and argue for the best possible deal you can get.

SBA Lending

By far, the most common and sought after source of business and franchise funding is through SBA Loan Programs. Why? Because the SBA will usually guarantee 75% to 85% of the loan for the lender. SBA 7(a) loans are the most common I encounter because we are not a high cost franchise and no real estate is involved.

NOTE

The SBA requires 10% of your own money (to demonstrate you've got skin in the game). The individual banks can, and often do, require more.

SBA 7(a) loan programs can be used for:

- Acquiring, refinancing, or improving real estate and buildings
- Short- and long-term working capital
- Refinancing business debt
- Purchasing equipment, furniture, or supplies
- Buying a new or existing franchise

The maximum loan amount for a 7(a) loan is $5 million. Key eligibility factors are based on what the business does to receive its income, its credit history, and where the business operates. Your lender will help you figure out which type of loan is best suited for your needs. For more on eligibility visit: SBA.Gov/Partners

You can use SBA's Lender Match tool to connect with a participating SBA lender. You will apply for your loan directly through your lender.

According to my colleague Matt Goers, VetFran Committee Member, Marine Veteran, and Senior Loan Officer, SBA loan rates vary based on loan size, term, collateral, down payment, and overall credit strength. For franchises under the 7(a) loan program, interest rates typically range from prime +2.25% to prime +2.75%, with both fixed and variable options. At the time of writing, variable rates max out at prime +6.5%—but negotiating even a minor rate reduction can impact your payments, so always ask about veteran discounts.

Recently, the SBA dropped its collateral threshold back to $350,000 from $500,000, meaning you will need to provide collateral for loans above $350,000. The SBA can take your house if it's the source of collateral and you default. However, some lenders may have stricter collateral demands, so shop around to find the best deal.

NOTE

Not all SBA-approved banks or credit unions will work with every borrower—many have their own lending criteria and preferred loan profiles. Smaller loans (under $200,000) are typically harder to secure because data shows higher failure rates for these amounts. While it might seem counterintuitive, lenders often prioritize larger loans since the paperwork for a $125,000 loan is the same as a $500,000 loan, making smaller loans less attractive to process.

Direct Franchisor Financing

This is not a common practice, but it is something that some franchisors offer; sometimes they'll finance some or all of the franchise fee. There may be other franchisor funding available, too. Take a look at ITEM 10 in the FDD for details.

Discounts

Many franchisors will offer discounts on their franchise fees for veterans. To be a member of VetFran, the franchisor must have been franchising for three years, meet certain other criteria, and offer a discount of 10% or more off of the franchise fee.

There may be other franchisor funding available, too. Take a look at ITEM 10 in the FDD for details.

NOTE

Full disclosure. G-FORCE is the one exception to the minimum 10% discount since we are exclusive to veterans and have no way of offering a special discount only for veterans. Our discounts are already baked in. Many thanks to the good folks at VetFran and the IFA for understanding our Catch-22 and making a reasonable exception.

You will also see veteran discounts from franchise brands that aren't members of VetFran. These discounts will be mentioned in their FDD. Discounts can save you thousands, but they will not be enough to finance your purchase. Occasionally, you may even find the franchise fee completely waived for veterans.

Alternative Financing and Grants

There's a common misconception that the VA or government automatically provides free money for veterans to start businesses. While there isn't a single universal grant waiting for veterans, there are targeted funding opportunities available—but they require research and effort to access.

For example, one of our franchise owners successfully secured $40,000 in funding through a State of Kansas special loan program at a fixed 4% interest rate, significantly lower than standard business loans. However, programs like this are often limited in availability and may run out of funds annually.

I once received $10,000 in funding through Massachusetts Fallen Heroes and InnoVets as part of a business pitch competition. Opportunities like this exist but require targeted applications, persistence, and strategy.

For years, I believed that free or low cost money for veterans to start businesses was largely a myth. Most of what I heard were vague rumors, and I rarely saw clear-cut programs that actually delivered funding. That changed when I met Kedma Ough at one of our annual conferences. Kedma isn't just someone who talks about funding—she's cracked the code on how to find it. As a nationally recognized funding strategist and the best-selling author of *Target Funding*, she has helped over 10,000 entrepreneurs identify hidden funding opportunities tailored to their specific needs—especially veterans.

Rather than relying on one-size-fits-all solutions, Kedma teaches a targeted approach, showing business owners how to unlock grants, specialized loans, state programs, and alternative capital sources based on their location, industry, background, and specific circumstances. Since learning from Kedma, I've come to realize that there is money out there—but you have to know where to look and how to access it. And, it's going to take a lot of work on your end to secure it.

Kedma teaches that funding is based on variables that are associated with you and your chosen business. *Target funding variables* are specific variables that can help you identify the funding options for your business.

Each variable may have a different avenue to target so it's very important to list the variables first. As a veteran, your service to the military is one variable that is automatic. However, there are other variables to consider including:

Here is a list of some important variables:

1. Geographic: Your business location will help identify any specific funds available from your state, county, city, or particular neighborhood. Check out your local city and state programs and see what they have to offer you.
2. Demographic: Gender-focused. If you identify as a women-owned business you may be eligible for funds set aside for women.
3. Demographic: Minority-owned.
4. Income level: Sometimes your income level works for you and not against you, even if you are living on the edge, paycheck by paycheck.
5. Service-disabled veterans.

Some of Kedma's Favorite Funding Resources:

Matched-Saving Grants:

One of her favorite programs that supports business owners who are building businesses is the Individual Development Account (IDA) program. IDAs are matched savings accounts for people with modest incomes used to achieve specific goals such as buying a home, getting post-secondary education, or beginning a business. IDAs vary from program to program, but the important commonality is that for every dollar you save the organization will match it. Sometimes IDAs provide a 2:1 match and sometimes they provide an 8:1 match. These can be very competitive to qualify for.

To find a potential IDA program near you, go to the website of Prosperity Now (prosperitynow.org), a national nonprofit organization focused on helping disadvantaged people achieve financial stability and navigate to the *Find an IDA Program* portal. There, you click on an interactive map of the United States for the names and contact information of IDA programs in your state. You will need to contact the IDA provider directly to learn more about and apply for an IDA program.

Angel Investors

An angel investor is someone with a high net worth who provides financial backing for small start-ups or entrepreneurs, typically in exchange for ownership equity in the company. Once again there are angel investor groups all over the country and the key is to target the right investor or investor group. Not all investors are right for you and one of the ways to find out is to review their investment thesis. Many accredited investors are aligned with specific investor groups. For example, Kedma belongs to TBD Angels (tbdangels.com), a group of angel investors who are current operators at leading start-ups and executives at major companies, with deep and varied experiences.

Service-Disabled Veterans

The Vocational Rehabilitation & Employment (VR&E) program of the U.S. Department of Veterans Affairs (VA) offers self-employment/business-ownership grants for service-disabled veterans. The VR&E self-employment grant, also known as the Chapter 31 program (Title 38 of the United States Code, Chapter 31), is a disability benefit through the Veterans Benefits Administration (VBA). It is available to all veterans who qualify and apply for a Chapter 31 grant. VR&E grants are used primarily to provide self-employment that is possible given the applicant's disabilities. Candidates for the VR&E self-employment track are assigned to either a Category I or Category II grant, based on the "severity of the disability and the limitations to employability."

A service-disabled veteran who owns an existing business may be entitled to a VR&E grant (Category I or II) if that vocation is unsuitable due to the vet's disability. In that case, funding may be provided for services to help the veteran overcome his/her impediments to employment in the existing business. Funding is generally for start-up only and *not* provided for expenditures relating solely to improving, updating, or expanding an existing suitable business.

VR&E grants of up to $25,000 can be approved by the veteran's local Vocational Rehabilitation Officer. Amounts greater than $25,000 require approval from the local Vocational Rehabilitation Director. Grant awards may be used for vocational training, rehabilitative services relating to the veteran's VR&E training and rehabilitation plan, business training, inventory, supplies, equipment, and/or business licenses and insurance.

In addition, every state vocational rehabilitation agency in the United States provides services that support the employment goals of people with disabilities, including self-employment. This assistance includes start-up grants to help pay for the costs of starting a business or establishing self-employment. Each state sets its own policies regarding the use of voc-rehab grants for self-employment. If you're interested in applying for a voc-rehab business grant, contact the vocational rehabilitation agency or department in your state and ask to speak to a VR counselor regarding funding and assistance to achieve self-employment or to start a small business. This is often a small monetary grant of between $5,000 and $10,000.

State Business Financing Programs Specifically Made for Small Businesses

Here is an example:

Illinois: Minority/Business/Disabled/Veteran Participation Loan Program. The MBDV PLP is administered by the Illinois Department of Commerce and Economic Opportunity (DCEO), which goes by the trade name Advantage Illinois. Available to Illinois-based small or midsize businesses majority-owned by an eligible individual with a disability. Loan: $200,000. (Interest rate not available.) Up to seven years repayment terms. Uses: Business procurement, start-ups, expansion.

Government Loan Programs for Veteran-Owned Businesses

Various state, county, and city governments around the country offer loan programs for veteran business owners, which typically offer more flexible terms than most conventional lenders. Two such lending programs are briefly described here, to give you an idea of what might be available in your area.

Colorado: Veteran Access Loan Opportunity Fund (VALOR)

VALOR is an initiative of the Colorado Enterprise Fund (CEF). Eligibility is for small businesses located in the state of Colorado that are majority owned by veterans who do not qualify for a business loan from a bank. Loan: Up to $500,000, term loan. Zero interest for up to six months, then discounted 2% from standard CEF interest rate. 1.3% loan initiation fee. Up to 10 years, repayment terms. Uses: Working capital, equipment, inventory, property improvements, business purchases, purchases of commercial real estate.

NOTE

Accion, the nation's largest nonprofit online lending network, operates four community development financial institutions (CDFIs) that serve small businesses throughout the country—including, as a priority objective, businesses owned by people with disabilities. Qualification requirements, loan amounts ($300 to $1 million), loan uses, repayment terms, interest rates, collateral requirements, and other terms and conditions depend upon the loan products offered by the individual CDFI. For more information, including which Accion location serves your state, visit the Accion U.S. website (accion.org).

Financing Conclusion

It is beyond the scope of this book to detail every possible funding option out there, but if there is anything I want you to take away from this chapter it is this: Do your homework, have an honest financial conversation with yourself before you start talking to family members, bankers, or anyone else. Be clear-eyed about your current circumstances and, if necessary, make a plan to improve your situation, especially as it relates to your credit score.

From there, know there is a wide range of options—some of which you won't touch because of your risk assessment, but others will align with your goals and tolerance for risk. I strongly recommend that you get a copy of Kedma Ough's book *Target Funding: A Proven System to Get the Money and Resources You Need to Start or Grow Your Business* to get a fuller sense of the possibilities. Head to kedmaough.com for more information.

One last thing before moving on, don't let your eyes glaze over talking about financing. It may not be part of your current wheelhouse, but you'll have to master it in order to have a chance at building your business whatever form that takes. There are people and resources out there to learn from if you need that help. I encourage you to take your time, be thorough, dig deep using the tools outlined in Kedma's book, and master the requirements of funding your dream.

CHAPTER 11

RESPONSIBLE FRANCHISING

The essential truth about the franchise model is this: We (franchisors and franchisees) sink or swim together. The business needs of the franchisor are met by the franchisees executing the plan. The business needs of the franchisees are met by working within the franchisor's system with the support they need to succeed. Everything I've mentioned in this book comes down to each and every party involved in the sales, support, and operation of a franchise being wholly responsible for their part in the success of the brand and the stakeholders.

As former military, you understand this concept. The strength of your squad hinged on the actions of each individual, the squad's actions fed the work of the platoon, the platoon to the company, the company to the battalion, and so on. At its root is the individual executing the plan based on training and the vision of leadership.

That's the trunk around which the franchise model branches out. That alone does not capture the depth and value of what a franchise opportunity can be for you.

Throughout this manual, I have emphasized the importance of continually taking stock of your own abilities, goals, expectations, and willingness to engage with the franchisor's model for your business. It costs you nothing to look in the mirror and assess who you are relative to the demands of business ownership. It costs you nothing, but it does require your time and honesty.

For the franchisor, nothing should matter more to them than finding qualified, engaged candidates to help them execute their growth plans using franchisor-provided training and support systems. And then, doing everything they can to help the new owner succeed.

The term "Responsible Franchising" has become the latest buzzword in the franchise world. It's a common sense approach to franchising, boiling down to simply doing what's right.

Sign me up.

Responsible Franchising is the industry response to concerns about bad actors and a much-feared push for legislation further regulating the industry.

Anyone and everyone in the franchise space can add their own thoughts on what they think defines Responsible Franchising. It's still a work in progress, but it's rapidly starting to come into focus.

Ever the skeptic, I'm just concerned it's going to turn into a PR catch-phrase and sales tool for some, rather than a commitment to truly abide by these principles. Overall, though, I'm very encouraged and view it as a positive.

Responsible Franchising sets realistic expectations on both sides of the transaction. It insists franchisors reinvest in support as they grow, as well as insisting franchisees come prepared to put in the work to grow their businesses.

Spotting a Responsible Franchisor

I asked my colleague, Joe Mathews (mentioned earlier), thought leader in the franchise arena and owner of The Franchise Performance Group, to offer a few insights from his book, *The Ultimate Guide to Responsible Franchising*.

Here's what Joe had to say:

> *Ask a franchisor what business they are in. While every franchisor distributes its own brand of products and services, franchising is a business unto itself.*
>
> *As you investigate franchises, you will find that brilliant business models are a dime a dozen. However, brilliant franchisors are few. It takes a brilliant franchisor to build a strong regional or national brand to add equity value to your investment. If you were to ask CEOs of franchise companies, "What business are you in?" you will probably hear about the products and services they distribute, such as, "I am in the auto repair business" or "I am in the home furnishings business." You will seldom hear, "I am in the franchising business."*
>
> *Before investing your savings in a franchise, you may want to make sure you're doing business with a responsible franchisor who knows they are in the business of recruiting, training, developing, resourcing, and leading a team of entrepreneurs to build a brand. While most people investigating franchises examine the franchisor's effectiveness in distributing their products and services, few people look to determine whether or not the franchisor is skilled in the business of franchising and lick their wounds later.*

Joe was also on a recent podcast with Erik Van Horn of *Franchise Secrets*. Joe makes another excellent point "The franchisor . . . is under a social obligation . . . a social contract, to add more value to the franchisee than they're extracting in continuing fees."

What Joe said!

Regulation on the Horizon?

I come from a career in the airlines, the most regulated industry that ever existed (after nuclear). That intense regulation helped create the environment for the safest form of travel in the world. It's a typical pilot joke to respond when asked what we do to say, "bus driver" or "heavy equipment operator." In recent years "aviation lawyer" became a popular wisecrack in recognition of the myriad regulations and laws that have to be followed just to get the jet pushed off the gate. Our flight plans could stretch 50' or more and we were responsible for every word of it.

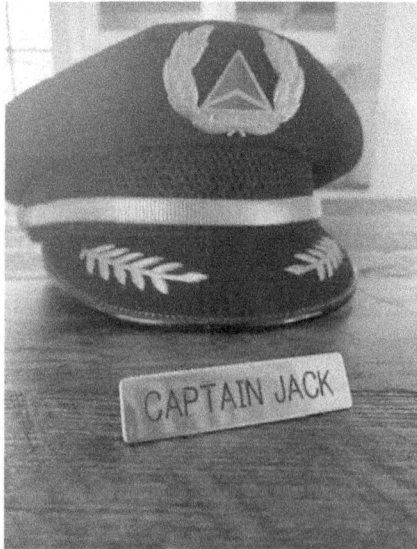

Narrator's voice: Captain Jack did not, in fact, read every word of the 50' flight plan.

While many of my colleagues in the franchise industry are panicking over proposed changes, I'm a firm believer that regulation done right is a very healthy and welcome change. The FTC Rule for Franchising absolutely needs updating. Regulation in the form of better transparency will increase the "safety" of buying into a franchise. I'm all for it.

Matthew Haller, president of the IFA, seeing legislation was imminent in California, was wisely proactive in partnering the IFA with the State of California to craft legislative language to add a broker's disclosure sheet, similar to the FDD, to all transactions involving brokers. Transparency is a good thing. Many believe licensing of brokers, similar to the real estate license process, is in order. I agree, but it's not my battle.

For the latest policy positions by the IFA on Responsible Franchising, visit franchise.org/responsible-franchising.

Next up, other opportunities in the franchise industry for veterans besides franchise ownership.

CHAPTER 12

OTHER OPTIONS FOR VETERANS IN FRANCHISING

While this book is designed for today's veterans looking into buying franchises, I would be remiss if I didn't bring up the wide range of other employment opportunities in this space.

The same enthusiasm for recruiting veterans as franchisees can be found for employment within many franchise organizations.

Just recently, using HireMilitary® and the Skillbridge program, I was able to recruit a new Chief Operating Officer, Jay Sperry, a former First Sergeant, fresh out of the Marines after 20 years and nine days (but, who's counting?). With zero experience in the franchise world, or business world for that matter, Jay has been the perfect fit for our team as he helps tighten up our systems, improves our four brand processes, enforces brand standards, and helps me chart the course for our future. With no prior business experience, I can say, without hesitation, his military experience translated perfectly to what we were seeking.

There are plenty of franchisors and thousands of franchisees who are looking for help in challenging and rewarding positions. Don't overlook this space!

To my fellow franchisors or franchisees, you should look to HireMilitary or other military job sources to help you fill key positions. Some candidates might even qualify for the SkillBridge program. This program gives separating military members up to six months to intern with you at no cost (except a finder's fee). Their salaries are paid by the U.S. government until they officially separate or retire. Don't overlook this incredible opportunity to bring talented veterans into the franchise space. You'll be glad you did.

Promise.

CHAPTER 13

TODAY'S VETERANS IN FRANCHISING

Back in CHAPTER 4, I gave you a brief overview of the veterans who built iconic brands and honed the franchising model. If I may, I'd like to give a shoutout to some of my fellow veterans making a difference in today's franchise industry outside of my own organization.

At the top of the list, I'll place Gordon Logan, mentioned earlier. No one discusses Veterans in Franchising these days without recognizing Gordon. With 1,900 Sport Clips locations, he is, by far, the most well-known veteran in today's world of franchising. He's a former Chairman of the IFA's VetFran program and serves on the VFW Foundation Board. Sport Clips is the primary sponsor of the Ageless Aviation Dreams Foundation which has six Stearman biplanes providing rides to veterans in assisted living homes. Gordon is a force for good in the franchise industry.

Speaking of Sport Clips, Cheston Syma, former Marine Platoon Sergeant, owns 50 of them. He also owns three Tommy's® Express Car Washes, one Semper® Laser Hair Removal, and has two Sweathouz® Contrast Therapy units in progress, with eight additional licenses signed. He is also in the process of launching 10 Big Blue® Swim School franchises in Texas over the next seven years and is founder of Wheelhouse Partners, a franchise management service. Cheston was chosen as the Veteran Entrepreneurship MVP for 2024 by Franchising.com. He's partnered with Edwin Greer, an Army veteran, on many of these projects.

Mary Kennedy Thompson, former Marine Corps officer, recently stepped down as COO of Neighborly, and is now CEO of BNI®, a networking franchise. Prior to her role at Neighborly, Mary served as President of the Mr. Rooter® franchise. Mary assumed the Chair of the IFA in early 2025.

Sean Falk, former captain in the Marines, is President and COO of Careertopia®, an executive search team focused on franchising, and serves on the VetFran committee.

Joshua Emison, mentioned earlier (the franchise bridge guy), is a Naval Academy grad, a former Marine officer, and worth a follow on LinkedIn for his franchise insights.

Victor Ulibarri, Air Force veteran, owns an Ace® Handyman Services franchise in New Mexico and already has 10 technicians working for him within his rookie year.

Joe DePinto, West Point grad, is the CEO of 7-Eleven®. He's kind of a big deal.

Allan Young, Army veteran, founded Shelf Genie® in 2007 and sold to Neighborly in 2017. He later launched the Art of Drawers® franchise concept in 2019.

Multi-unit Ziebart® franchise owner Mark Mattiacio served in the Marines from 2009 through 2013.

Dustin Ingle, nine-year veteran of the Army, is the founder of the Insulation Commandos® franchise. Launched in 2023, their website lists 12 locations with more in the works.

Navy veteran Michael Quilty founded Wild Bill's® Craft Beverage

Company in 2018. Like VSB, they franchise exclusively to fellow veterans.

Bryan Park, Air Force veteran and graduate of the Air Force Academy, is founder and CEO of Footprints® Flooring franchise. They now have over 150 franchise locations nationwide.

Tanner Harris, former Navy pilot and currently a pilot with United® Airlines, is the founder of Blue Nose® Aerial Imaging, a drone franchise. He ruined my record for being the only airline pilot to become a franchisor. No sour grapes whatsoever, Tanner!

Evan Greco, former Army officer, is Brand President and a franchisee of Rolling Suds®, a pressure washing business.

Matt Goers, former Marine Sergeant, is a Senior Vice President of First Bank of the Lake, an active SBA lender for small businesses. He assisted me with the chapter on financing and he's another member of the VetFran committee.

Mike and Dave McCloskey, Iraq war veterans, operate G.I. HAUL.® Junk Removal as franchisors.

Jimmy Weeks, Air Force veteran, is CEO and Founder of Internet Strategy Labs, which provides analytics to the franchise community. Jimmy is active with VetFran and assisted me with getting G-FORCE accepted by them. I conduct an interview with Jimmy in the next chapter so he may share his unique insights with you.

I want to share that conversation with you because it is a good reminder there are inspiring people working behind the scenes on your behalf, dedicating themselves to helping veterans like you discover if franchising is the right fit for you, and then being there to support your efforts as you grow your business. I promise you Jimmy's insights are invaluable.

Final thoughts on all these modern day veterans making their way in the franchising world. There are certainly many, many more than this short list worthy of inclusion that I'm just simply unaware of. There exists no directory of all franchise positions held by veterans. This exercise was merely intended to give you a small sampling of what's happening out there.

Now, on to my conversation with Jimmy. When Jimmy talks, people listen.

NOTE

For those of you old enough to remember the wildly successful E.F. Hutton commercials from the late '70s through the early '80s using that expression, here's my last annoying comment on this topic of veterans everywhere—Hutton was a Korean War veteran!

CHAPTER 14

INTERVIEW WITH JIMMY WEEKS

Jimmy Weeks is an Air Force veteran and CEO/Founder of Internet Strategy Labs. He is part of the VetFran committee and a trusted friend and colleague. The interview that follows has been lightly edited for clarity.

First, can you give us a little bit about your military background and how you wound up involved in franchising and VetFran?

I signed up for the Air Force as a junior in high school and had a guaranteed job. Typical small town upbringing and wanted out of town. Was bullied on the regular and while I could have gone to college on an academic scholarship, I wasn't interested in college and more bullying. While working in hospitals as a medical admin, I was able to go to school and received two degrees with web design and illustration secondary to a BS in medical administration.

After 12 1/2 years in the military, I started my own web design business that grew to an agency. Our start in franchising was web development, SEO, and advanced analytics for some of the largest brands on the planet. KFC, Pizza Hut, Meineke all became amazing case studies for our use of analytics, heatmapping, and SEO prowess helping brands grow.

In 2014, we subsequently converted to a SaaS platform and marketing analytics dashboard specific to the unique multi-location franchise models. It took several years to break into the trusted inner circle of franchising and earn a seat on the VetFran committee. Bringing together my love for the military and my love for franchising is an amazingly rewarding career.

What do you like most about franchising?

Being involved in uplifting and supporting brands to grow and complete their mission is very rewarding! When brands grow, it's new franchise owners, their families, their communities, and more jobs in that community. It is a very profound snowball effect and being part of that process is amazing!

Least?

No matter what industry you're in, there can be predatory activities and franchising is no different. Companies targeting military members definitely occurs. Fortunately, there are groups like VetFran and individuals like Jack who embrace advocacy roles and help veterans navigate business ownership.

Tell us about some success stories you're aware of from the franchisee perspective.

I think my favorite is Cheston Syma, a minority veteran who owns dozens of Sport Clips franchise locations across two states. Cheston wasn't a lifer and didn't have a retirement—instead he started with a business partner. Cheston is a perfect illustration of the opportunities available to someone who doesn't have big investment dollars. Honed leadership and organization skills coupled with the confidence to grow will take you a long way.

Any failures?

Unfortunately, I just heard from a veteran friend that I worked with 30 years ago and found out he purchased a brick and mortar pizza franchise. His location and business failed and he is in bankruptcy. While he did several things wrong, it's a typical outcome if you don't have or utilize all the support that is available. VetFran has a monthly "Franchising 101 for Veterans" webinar; if he had seen this prior, or had a copy of this Field Manual, his story would be different. He and his wife created a book of notes they will use moving forward. They're dusting themselves off and will be armed to the teeth as they move toward their next franchise opportunity.

What do you think our fellow vets can do to improve their chances for success?

First, reach out for support from organizations and people that have mastered what you haven't. Find the experts and follow their guidance. Secondly, don't overextend yourself when investing in a business. Start with a smaller concept/investment and then grow in territories or other concepts. It's easier/safer to expand and diversify than to go all in! Nobody needs that kind of stress. Lastly, follow your gut and that little voice in your head. If you're too stressed about a decision, it could be that it's not the right one.

How can a novice to the franchise world sort through so many options and make the right choice?

Find a concept type that matches your budget and investment level. A retail store or restaurant is incredibly challenging, but a home-based concept can open very quickly. Once you find your concept type, compare no less than three franchise systems in terms of fees, investment ranges, financial performance, and how long it would take to make your investment back.

Finally, what do you wish you knew "then" that you know now?

I wish I would have understood I could find, afford, and excel in franchise ownership. With 30+ years as an entrepreneur and all the ups and downs of a business start-up, I am supremely confident that my hard work in a franchise system(s) would have definitely yielded more revenue and happiness for myself and my family.

CHAPTER 15

FRANCHISE OR DIY?

The matter of whether to buy a franchise or strike out on your own has more than enough content for another book. But, for our purposes here, I'll simply touch on some major points for you to consider.

I opened and closed a couple of businesses long ago that never really worked. I learned the hard way that starting a business is really easy. Starting a successful business is another matter entirely.

Those who are striking out on their own greatly underestimate what it takes to launch a business properly, let alone run one successfully. Many seem to think simply filing for their LLC, building a website, and having business cards printed will cause the customers to beat a path to their door. Nothing could be further from the truth.

Time after time in my local community I see common mistakes being repeated over and over, as it's clear the well-meaning new owners have no idea how to brand, market, advertise, or capture market share.

I see the same thing across the country as I follow competitor activity in Facebook groups we share. Each of the services offered by our four brands has a fairly low barrier to entry, yet many of the independents struggle to find work. That's not to say independents can't crush it.

Some are, but it's typically a longer and heavier lift on their own. Many fail. The marketplace always wins.

Technology is tougher and more expensive to keep up with for independents than franchise systems, too. Franchises can scale. Independents can't scale very easily. Think about the buying power of a national brand. Our costs per location for website support and tech is a fraction of that compared to an independent. Layer in the authority Google will attribute to a multi-unit brand with locations across the country compared to a single unit.

With benefit of hindsight, if I only knew then what I know now I would have absolutely bought into a franchise system 25 years ago. At the time, I thought franchising was only for those with really deep pockets. Who knows where I'd be today? Multi-unit owner? Certainly. Multi-brand owner? Likely. Retired? Probably.

If you do decide to strike out on your own, I'll offer this one bit of advice: Please, choose your company name and brand very carefully and avoid the common trap of simply using your initials or your and your partner's initials. I've spent more than a few hours at the Secretary of State's office in New Hampshire registering my various business names watching countless others use the same failed formula over and over and over again.

Was it "R&M" or "R&N"? "B&L" or "D&L"? More than likely, customers won't remember one or both of the initials.

Also, don't use common superlatives like *deluxe, elite, premiere, quality,* etc. These names have zero meaning to consumers.

Facts: No one remembers initials. No one remembers superlatives.

Branding is everything!

Enough said on that topic.

"A Franchise Is the Cheapest Partner You Can Find"

That's a quote from my colleague Joshua Emison (mentioned earlier in the franchise bridge analogy), and I think he's exactly right.

What other "partner" lets you join forces for $30,000 to $60,000 (average franchise fees), shares responsibility for your success, has an entire support staff that you hire for pennies on the dollar (your royalties) compared to doing it yourself, is responsible for creating all the marketing and branding materials, gives you buying power, hands you national account work (some brands anyway), and lets you keep 100% ownership of your business profits? Only one—the franchisor.

Even the top performers in my brands, those who pay the most in royalties, have a bargain. When they factor in what they might pay for only one or two good employees, they can enjoy the benefits of having multiple staff members at their disposal, "free" representation at trade shows trying to recruit new business, no worries about tech, marketing, graphics, etc., and so much more.

I'd also like to add some comments on this topic from a franchise colleague of mine, Christian Dudulak, of Franchise Sidekick.

> *Franchising is the most democratic wealth creation vehicle in human history, yet it's the least talked about.*
>
> *What other investment can you . . .*
>
> *1. Buy with leverage—buy/build an asset for 20% to 30% down and finance the rest.*
>
> *2. Invest in an asset for as little as $100,000 to $250,000+ ($25,000 to $63,000 out-of-pocket).*
>
> *3. Have the potential to experience YOY growth of 10%, 20%, 30%, 100%+.*
>
> *4. And, have the potential to net 15% to 30% on what could*

grow into $500,000 to $1 million+ in annual revenue (depending on the brand).

NOTE

The numbers above reflect Christian's opinions, not necessarily the author's (doing my best to avoid franchise jail by not making an earnings claim). But I agree with his overall message.

Done right, franchising is absolutely 100% the way to go versus going it alone, in my humble opinion.

Chapter 16

Final Thoughts

Now, the Telling You What I Told You Part

You now have had a crash course (and a few simulator crashes) in franchising covering what a franchise is, the franchise world itself, and all the players inside that ecosystem (and how they impact and interact with you). I've shared how veterans have made franchising what it is today, tackled some myths about franchising, and offered up how I would read the FDD (emphasis on ITEM 20!). I've added information about finding the right franchise for you, financing options, Responsible Franchising, and other opportunities in the franchise industry for veterans as well as included a shoutout to some fellow veterans making a difference, an interview with the legendary Jimmy Weeks (one of the nicest guys you'll ever meet), and a comparison of DIY versus franchising.

Whew!

We've covered a lot of ground in this manual. If you've come this far, I hope you feel it was worth your while. My goal was not to scare you away from franchising but to steer you away from the *wrong* franchise decision. I've placed useful and practical information in your hands regarding the franchise world—information that comes from over 14 years' experience as a franchisor, the last seven of which have been to offer franchises exclusively to my fellow veterans.

I hope I have provided you with an insider's view of franchising and the risks and rewards of becoming a business owner through franchising. Again, I have nothing to sell you, and I'm not offering legal advice. This is just my view from 30,000'.

I guarantee you will surprise the brokers and franchisors with your insight from this manual. I would love feedback on those conversations!

If there is one single takeaway I want you to have it is this: Do your homework. Just as no one did your PT for you, you have to take charge of your inquiry into franchising. If you leave it for others to do on your behalf, no matter how well-meaning and professional they are, you are ceding your responsibility for your decisions.

There is simply no excuse to not come prepared.

The effort you put into preparation, to understanding the terms of franchising and the various models and markets, will make this process less opaque, with fewer opportunities to be caught off guard by any of it.

Your history of service, your military training, your understanding of teams and processes, of executing the plan, separates you as a prospective franchisee. I am biased in favor of supporting the efforts of veterans to become business owners as they look to secure their financial futures. Looking back, I wish I had pursued owning a franchise much earlier instead of other choices I made.

Service. Integrity. Pride.

Those are the three core values of Veteran Service Brands and our four franchise brands.

Service: in recognition of our prior service to our country, turned now into serving our communities.

Integrity: operating at the highest level of integrity and honesty with our franchise partners, vendors, and end customers.

Pride: taking pride in all we do, making things right when they go wrong.

We don't hold the monopoly on those words. I'm 100% certain service, integrity, and pride resonate within you. You can—no, *must*—bring those very same values and many others you possess to the welcoming arms of the franchise world should you choose to become a franchise owner.

Last Words

Should you decide to enter franchising you'll be standing on the shoulders of giants—men and women who served their country and, over time, paved a remarkable path to economic freedom and prosperity for those willing to take the risk and work at it with the same dedication and purpose as the military offered.

Giants.

It humbles me every day to know I am part of that continuum and I hope this Field Manual helps you decide what is best for you. No one can promise you success, but your fellow veterans have set the standards for the industry regarding the well-being of their franchisees, employees of those franchisees, and the communities they serve. In addition to not going it alone as a franchisee, you'll be in the company of other vets, some long gone, others now making hay, who put their military training and experience to work in civilian life and their mentorship is always at hand. You just have to look.

At the back of the manual you'll find five appendices and a Glossary of Terms for your reference.

I'd welcome your feedback as to how this manual may have helped you and what areas I may have overlooked that you would like to see covered in the next edition.

I'm already planning that second edition to capture veteran stories I may have overlooked, past and present, in the franchising world. Shoot me an email if you have names you'd like me to include in the next edition.

Finally, I do thank you for your service (even though it's an overused phrase, it still matters) and wish you nothing but the best on your entrepreneurial journey.

Salute!

Appendix 1: What It Takes To Be a Rock Star Franchisee

1. Follow the system. The system works if you work the system. Don't fight the system you just bought into.
2. Devote the necessary time to the enterprise—whatever it takes to get it rolling.
3. Be a sponge (gather info from multiple sources).
4. Participate in any and all coaching calls, group calls, etc. (key word "participate").
5. Plan to spend more than the minimum outlined in the FDD on ads and then spend it.
6. Speed wins—if you're in the service industry, make sure calls are answered, quotes processed quickly, and services provided efficiently.
7. Communicate, communicate, communicate:

   A. With your customers
   B. With your franchisor
   C. With your staff
   D. With your fellow franchisees

8. Ask for a mentor from within the franchisee group.

9. Invest in your staff to include good wages and training.
10. Attend the annual conference and participate at a level outside your comfort zone.
11. Report on time and pay your royalties on time.
12. Give more than you take (it always rebounds to you).
13. Take an interest in your fellow franchise owners' success.
14. Offer your franchisor feedback (good and bad) on what's happening at your location.
15. Stay positive.
16. Join the local chamber and/or other networking groups.
17. Engage in your community.
18. Pay your vendors promptly.
19. Don't forget where you started and who got you there.
20. Keep clean books for your eventual exit.
21. Take time for your family and yourself.
22. Embrace the suck.

Appendix 2: Questions To Ask the Franchisor

1. How did you become a franchisor?
2. What is your brand's Unique Selling Proposition (USP) for prospective franchisees?
3. What's the USP for your franchisees' customers?
4. Who are your major franchise competitors from your perspective?
5. Who are your major competitors from your franchisees' perspective?
6. What are your system strengths?
7. What is training like?
8. What is your marketing plan for franchisees?
9. Tell me about your tech stack (strengths and weak spots).
10. What are your weaknesses (and how are you addressing those)?
11. What's your growth plan?
12. Is your territory size adequate to support a single unit and allow for growth? What are some opportunities you see that haven't been pursued yet?
13. Is it hard to find employees in this sector? If so, what do you do to help?

14. What happened to your franchisees during COVID? Did you make any allowances to help them during this period?
15. Tell me about your top performers and bottom performers.
16. What is your franchisee failure rate? What do you attribute these failures to?
17. Any terminations not listed in the current FDD? If there are, please explain.
18. What can I expect to earn? Do a deeper dive in ITEM 19 with them. If they make no earnings claims, ask them why.
19. What would you say is your level of franchisee satisfaction? How many would buy it again? (Should be 80% or higher)
20. What do you think are your franchisees' biggest challenges?
21. For brick and mortar: What assistance do you provide with real estate and buildouts?
22. Tell me about any litigation.
23. What keeps you up at night?
24. What does it take to be a rock star franchisee in your system?

Appendix 3: Questions To Ask Current Franchisees

1. How did you become a franchisee?
2. What's your background?
3. What's your brand's Unique Selling Proposition (USP) for prospective franchisees?
4. What's the USP for your customers?
5. Who are your local and national competitors, from your perspective?
6. What are the brand/system strengths?
7. What are the brand's weaknesses (and how are they addressing those)?
8. What was training like?
9. Does the marketing plan provided by the franchisor work?
10. Tell me about your tech stack (strengths and weak spots).
11. What's your own growth plan?
12. Is your territory size adequate to support a single unit and allow for growth? What are some opportunities that you see that haven't been pursued yet?
13. Were you a franchisee during COVID? If so, how did that impact you? Did the franchisor make any allowances to help you during this period?

14. Tell me about the top performers and bottom performers in the system.
15. What can I expect to earn?
16. How long before you were cash flow positive?
17. What would you say is your level of franchisee satisfaction? Would you buy it again? (Should be 80% or higher system-wide)
18. What are your biggest challenges? What keeps you up at night?
19. For brick and mortar: What assistance do they provide with real estate and buildouts?
20. Tell me about your perspective on any litigation issues past or pending.
21. Are existing franchisees buying up more territory? (If yes, that's a good sign of a healthy brand)
22. What does it take to be a rock star franchisee in your system?

Appendix 4: Questions for Your Franchise Broker-Coach-Consultant and/or Advisor

1. How long have you been a broker?
2. What is your business background?
3. Have you ever owned a franchise? If not, why not?
4. How many franchisees have you placed?
5. Do you stay in touch with those you placed?
6. How many are successful and happy?
7. How many have failed? Any lessons learned from that? May I call them?
8. How many brands in your network?
9. Are you allowed to present offerings outside your network?
10. Are you willing to present offerings with lower commissions if it's a better fit for me?
11. Regarding brands they present: Ask them what due diligence they have done on their own.
12. Once you get very interested in a particular brand, ask them what their commission is.
13. Would they be willing to offer a rebate or credit toward a purchase? Expect pushback. What's the worst that can happen? Shave your head and send you to the Army? Too late for that.

Appendix 5: Glossary of Terms

Provided by Michael Seid of MSA Worldwide,
Army Veteran, member of the Board of Directors at IFA, and former
Chairman of VetFran

NOTE

I did not use all the terms within this Glossary. Some are for reference only.

Acknowledgement of Receipt: ITEM 23 of the Franchise Disclosure Document (FDD) that is signed by the prospective franchisee and provided to the franchisor (in hard copy or electronically signed) as proof of the date the FDD was received by the prospect.

Advertising Fee: An amount paid by the franchisee to the franchisor as a contribution to the franchise system's advertising fund(s). The fund is typically established to pay for the creation and placement of advertising and is used to offset the franchisor's administrative costs relating to "retail/brand" advertising. Payments are typically calculated as a percentage of gross sales.

Agent: A party that has implied or express (oral or written) authority to act on the behalf of another.

Approved Advertising Materials: Materials provided by the franchisor for the franchisee's use in their local market, or materials created by the franchisee which the franchisor has approved for use.

Approved Products: Specified products which a franchisee must buy for use in their business. Franchisor may also specify an authorized supplier (see authorized supplier definition below). Generally established to control the quality of the products used or sold by the franchisee in conducting their business.

Approved Site: A location that the franchisor determines will satisfactorily meet its criteria. Site approval by franchisor is generally not an indication of the sales potential or success of the location.

Arbitration: A method of resolving disputes.

Area Franchise: A franchise relationship that allows the franchisee to open multiple locations, usually in a defined territory within a pre-agreed upon timeline. Area franchisees usually pay an area fee for the rights granted by the franchisor.

Authorized/Designated Supplier: A supplier of products and/or services used in the operation of the franchise that has been approved by the franchisor to sell to franchisees. May be the franchisor or an affiliate company.

Broker: An outside salesperson or firm that undertakes, for a fee or commission, the sale of franchises for a franchisor. Franchise brokers are disclosed within the offering circular (franchise disclosure document). Some brokers like to call themselves franchise consultants, but this is a misnomer (see franchise consultant definition below).

Business Format Franchising (BFF): A franchise occurs when a business (the franchisor) licenses its trade name (the brand) and its operating methods (its system of doing business) to a person or group (the franchisee) that agrees to operate according to the terms of a contract (the franchise agreement). The franchisor provides the franchisee with support and, in some cases, exercises some control over the way the franchisee operates under the brand. In exchange, the franchisee usually pays the franchisor an initial fee (called a franchise fee) and a continuing fee (known as a royalty) for the use of the trade name and operating methods. BFF describes the system of delivery, not the specific product or service associated with the delivery as in Product or Trademark Franchising.

Business Plan: A planning document that details the objectives for the business and establishes processes and measures for meeting those objectives.

Capital Required: The initial investment or required amount of investment necessary to conduct the business.

Certification: Program by which franchisor or its franchisee may test and attest to the ability of an employee to perform certain job functions within the franchisee's business to the franchisor's standards. Certification can generally be revoked if the employee fails to maintain standards in performing the job function.

Churning: A failing location acquired by the franchisor and resold to a franchisee even though the franchisor felt that the location had a high chance of failure regardless of ownership. While churning is not a common occurrence in franchising today, it does occur, and sometimes a single location may be churned several times.

Company-Owned Location: A location, owned and operated by the franchisor, usually identical in appearance and operations to those of the system's franchises. While not required, most company-owned locations contribute to the system's advertising fund(s).

Copyright: The right to use and license others to use intellectual property, such as system manuals or other published materials.

Continuous Training: Training provided by franchisors to its franchisees, unit management, and staff, subsequent to the initial training provided.

Conversion Franchise: The conversion of an existing business within the franchisor's industry into the franchise system. Sometimes includes experienced operators without operating locations.

Culture of Compliance: Company culture whereby franchisees and staff do what is right for the system based on a feeling or knowledge that it is the right thing to do within the company philosophy, rather than because it is in the agreement or because someone is watching.

Days: Unless otherwise stated, days generally refer to calendar days.

Day-to-Day Management: As an independent owner, the franchisee is obligated to manage the day-to-day affairs of their business to meet the franchisor's brand standards.

Default: The failure of either party to meet the terms of the agreement. In franchising, certain defaults are enumerated and some can be cured in a defined period, while others may not be curable.

Design: The trade dress used by the franchise system for the franchise locations, including logo, layout, color scheme, signage, etc.

Disclosure Document: Also known as the Franchise Disclosure Document (FDD). Formerly known as the Uniform Franchise Offering Circular (UFOC). The format of the FDD is specified by the FTC and NASAA (federal and state regulators) and provides information about the franchisor, the obligations of the franchisor and the franchisee, fees, start-up costs, and other required information about the franchise system. It includes a listing of current and former franchisees. In addition to the disclosure portion of the FDD, the document will contain the franchise and other agreements and exhibits. It does not typically include unit earnings information.

Distributorship: The right granted by a manufacturer or wholesaler to sell their products.

Exclusive (Protected) Territory: A geographic area which provides the franchisee with certain rights, which may include exclusive operation. Franchisors may include carve-out provisions within an exclusive territory which define an excluded type of location (malls, airports, stadiums, arenas, supermarkets, hospitals, etc.).

Feasibility Study: An examination of the potential of a company to franchise, or of the potential success of a unit within a specific market or specific location.

Federal Trade Commission (FTC): The agency of the U.S. government which regulates franchising under FTC Rule 436.

Field Representative: Typically an employee of the franchisor responsible for ensuring compliance by the franchisee with system standards. Also responsible for providing assistance to franchisees in the operation of their businesses. May be a commissioned Area Representative.

Financial Performance Representation (FPR): Formerly known as an Earnings Claim, an FPR is the ITEM 19 representation of unit performance by a franchisor.

Footprint: Layout of a location including placement of all furniture, fixtures, and equipment.

Franchise: A relationship, as defined by the FTC and various states, which typically includes three basic elements: (1) the granting of the right to use the systems mark, (2) substantial assistance or control provided by the franchisor to the franchisee, (3) the payment of a fee (in excess of $500) during a period of time six months before or six months following the commencement of the relationship.

Franchise Agreement: The agreement between the franchisor and franchisee which specifies the obligations of each party to the other during and following the franchise relationship.

Franchise Attorney: A lawyer specializing in, or with significant knowledge of, the laws, regulations, and customs governing franchising.

Franchise Consultant: A business specialist with significant knowledge of the design, development, and operation of franchising and the underlying franchise relationship. Not to be confused with a broker, who is a sales agent for the franchisor (see Broker definition above).

Franchise Fee: The initial fee paid by the franchisee to the franchisor, usually upon signing the franchise agreement, as consideration for joining the system. Typically a flat payment as opposed to a percentage royalty and is used to offset a franchisor's franchisee start-up costs, marketing for franchisees, and other corporate expenses.

Franchisee: The person or company granted the rights (license) to do business under the trademark and trade name by the franchisor.

Franchisee in Good Standing: Franchisee operating their location and business in material compliance with franchisor's operating standards and current with all payments owed to franchisor and key suppliers.

Franchising: An indirect method of distribution; in other words, a method of growth.

Franchisor: A person or company which grants the license to a third party for the conducting of a business under their marks.

Gray Marketing: When a franchisee purchases under franchisor's negotiated agreements and uses the product or merchandise in another business or sells products or merchandise to another company.

Gross Sales: When used in franchising, generally the total sales of the business before the collection of any sales taxes and after specified deductions. Generally used as the basis for percentage royalty calculations.

Initial Investment: The total estimated cost for establishing the business, including the franchise fee, initial fixed assets and leasehold improvements, inventory, deposits, other fees and costs, and the working capital required during the initial start-up period (three months).

International Franchise Association (IFA): The industry trade association representing franchising. The IFA is based in Washington, D.C. www.franchise.org.

Internet Sales: Any sale initiated and completed on the world wide web.

Inquiry: Anyone requesting information about the franchise opportunity, whether via the web, by telephone, by fax, or by other methods.

Key Supplier or Vendor: Supplier with whom franchisor has negotiated pricing or product availability and whose products or services are an integral part of the franchise system.

Lead: An inquiry that is prequalified after the initial interview with a member of the franchisor's development staff as meeting the minimum criteria to become a franchisee, and who is invited to submit a franchise application.

Location: The site of the franchised or company-owned operation.

Manuals: The reference literature published by the franchisor which specifies the method of operating the business under the mark. The operations manual(s) enables the franchisor to alter and evolve the business.

Market Introduction Program: Marketing, advertising, and public relations activities used to launch the franchisee's location.

Master Franchisee: A franchise relationship which is granted for the development of a specified area and which allows the master franchisee to sub-franchise to other franchisees within the specified territory.

Multi-Unit Developer: A franchisee who agrees to open two or more locations, generally in a defined market over an agreed upon period of time.

Operating Principal: A single individual authorized by a franchise owner to make decisions on behalf of the franchisee. This person is the operating principal and is usually the person with whom the franchisor consults regarding the operation and conduct of the franchise.

Product and Trade Name Franchising: The licensing of a franchisee/dealer to sell or distribute a specific product using the franchisor's trademark, trade name, and logo (e.g., automobile or truck dealerships, farm equipment, mobile homes, gasoline service stations, automobile accessories, soda, beer, bottling). Describes the specific product or service associated with the delivery, not the system of delivery as with Business Format Franchising.

Protected or Exclusive Territory: Protection or exclusivity granted to a franchisee by the franchisor against the opening of company, franchisee, or other locations within the territory assigned to the franchisee.

Prospect: A person who has expressed interest in continuing the approval process by completing and submitting the franchise application and whose application has been preliminarily approved by the approval committee or the development director.

Quality Standards: The standards specified by the franchisor for the operation of the business. Quality standards are specified in the operations manuals, and quality franchise systems tightly control their standards for the benefit of the franchise system and its franchisees.

Registration: A requirement to submit the franchisor's disclosure document prior to the approval to offer franchises within some states. There is no requirement to register a franchise at the federal level. Registration is not an indication of state sanction of the value of the franchise offering.

Registration States: The various states that require franchisors to submit their FDD for approval prior to offering franchises. The registration states are members of NASAA.

Royalty Fee: Typically a percentage of gross sales paid by the franchisee to the franchisor on a regular basis. May also be a fixed or other fee basis.

Service Mark: A mark used to identify the services of one company as distinguished from the services of another. Service Marks are afforded similar protection to registered marks under the law.

Single-Unit Franchisee: Franchisee who owns and operates a single location.

Start-Up Costs (Initial Investment): The initial investment that the franchisee will make in becoming a franchisee. It is also known as an ITEM 7 disclosure. Generally includes the franchise fee, the cost of fixed assets, leasehold improvements, inventory, deposits, other fees and costs, and working capital required during the start-up period.

Success: As used in franchising, the absence of failure or closing of a location. It does not relate to unit sales or profitability.

Successor Agreement: Franchisee's ability to continue in the business for additional terms following a successful completion of their initial term.

System Brand Fund: A fund established and managed by franchisor to which all franchised and usually all company-owned units contribute monies to be spent on promoting and protecting the franchisor's brand. Frequently called an advertising fund.

Trademark: The mark, name, and logo which identifies the franchisor, and which is licensed by the franchisor for use by the franchisee.

Turnkey: A term used to describe a location which is provided to a franchisee fully equipped and ready to operate.

NOTES

1. WHAT IS A FRANCHISE?

1. Title 16 of C.F.R. § 436.1(h)
2. Strahota, H. (September 8, 2007) Franchise Development. *Benjamin Franklin: Father of Franchising?* Retrieved from https://www.franchise.org/franchise-informa tion/franchise-relations/benjamin-franklin-father-of-franchising
3. Singer Corporate. History of Singer. Retrieved from https://www.singer.com.tr/en/corporate/history
4. Dicke, T.S. (1992) *Franchising in America: The Development of a Business Method* (page 54). University of North Carolina Press
5. Sammarco, A.M. (2013) *A History of Howard Johnson's: How a Massachusetts Soda Fountain Became an American Icon* (page 15). American Palate, a division of The History Press

2. THE WORLD OF FRANCHISING

1. International Franchise Association. (February 14, 2024) Franchise Business Outlook. Retrieved from https://www.franchise.org/franchise-information/franchise-business-outlook/2024-franchising-economic-outlook
2. International Franchise Association. (2014) Veterans in Franchising: A Progress Report. Retrieved from https://www.franchise.org/sites/default/files/2019-06/Vet-Fran%20Progress%20Report%202014.pdf
3. Fitts, D. (November 1, 2023) Veterans. Veterans Join The Franchise Industry in Growing Numbers. Retrieved from https://www.franchise.org/franchise-informa tion/veterans/veterans-join-the-franchise-industry-in-growing-numbers
4. Neighborly. (November 15, 2024) Serving Those Who Served: A Guide to Veteran Friendly Franchises. Retrieved from https://franchise.neighborly.com/blog/a-guide-to-veteran-friendly-franchises
5. Miller, A. (2024) *Big Money in Franchising: Scaling Your Business in the Era of Private Equity* (page 17). Figure 1 Publishing, Inc
6. Franchising.com. (2023) 2023 Mega 99 Rankings. Retrieved from https://www.fran chising.com/articles/2023_mega_99_rankings.html

3. FRANCHISE MODELS

1. 1. Lazo, A. (January 6, 2010) Los Angeles Times "Obituary: Arthur E. Bartlett Dies at 76; Co-founder of Century 21"

4. VETERANS IN FRANCHISING

1. Historicmissourians.com. "Dale Carnegie." Retrieved from https://historicmissouri ans.shsmo.org/dale-carnegie

2. Biography.com. (September 14, 2022) "Conrad Hilton." Retrieved from https://www.biography.com/business-leaders/conrad-hilton

3. Wikipedia.com. "Charles D. Tandy." Retrieved from https://en.wikipedia.org/wiki/Charles_D._Tandy

4. Sammarco, A.M. (2013) *A History of Howard Johnson's: How a Massachusetts Soda Fountain Became an American Icon.* American Palate, a division of The History Press

5. Wheaton.edu. Marion E. Wade Center. "Marion E. Wade." Retrieved from https://www.wheaton.edu/academics/academic-centers/wadecenter/about/history/biographies/marion-e-wade/

6. Americacomesalive.com. "Tom Carvel: King of Soft-Serve." Retrieved from https://americacomesalive.com/tom-carvel-king-of-soft-serve

7. Marshall, I. (December 23, 2007) "Obituary: Irl H. Marshall" *Chicago Tribune.* Retrieved from https://www.chicagotribune.com/2007/12/23/death-notice-irl-h-marshall-jr-2/

8. Fundinguniverse.com. "The Steak 'n Shake Company History." Retrieved from https://www.fundinguniverse.com/company-histories/the-steak-n-shake-company-history/

9. Washingtonpost.com. (May 31, 2019) "Obituary: Curtis Blake, Co-Founder of the Friendly's Ice Cream Chain, dies at 102." Retrieved from https://www.washington post.com/local/obituaries/curtis-blake-co-founder-of-the-friendlys-ice-cream-chain-dies-at-102/2019/05/31/bc0a502c-83b2-11e9-95a9-e2c830afe24f_story.html

10. Carr, K. (September 1, 2014) *Fayetteville Observer.* "War and Donuts: Krispy Kreme." Retrieved from https://www.fayobserver.com/story/news/2014/09/01/war-doughnuts-krispy-kreme/22164761007/

11. Findagrave.com. "Emmett Joseph Culligan." Retrieved from https://www.finda grave.com/memorial/32470109/emmett-joseph-culligan

12. Ownby, C. (May 3, 2023) *Illinois Farm Bureau.* "The World of Swirled: Illinois' Original Dairy Queen." Retrieved from https://ilfbpartners.com/family/the-world-of-swirled-illinois-original-dairy-queen

13. Dickeys.com. "Our Story." Retrieved from https://www.dickeys.com/company/our-story

14. Malnic, E. (January 12, 2018) *Los Angeles Times.* "Obituary: Carl Karcher, 90, entrepreneur turned a hot dog stand into a fast food empire." Retrieved from https://www.latimes.com/local/obituaries/la-me-karcher12jan12-story.html

15. NNDB.com. "Burt Baskin." Retrieved from https://www.nndb.com/people/979/000178445/ Historylink.org. "Robbins, Irvine (1917-2008)." Retrieved from https://www.historylink.org/File/22911

16. Need Stafford, L. (September 8, 2014) *The Atlanta Journal Constitution.* "Truett Cathy through the years." Retrieved from https://www.ajc.com/business/truett-cathy-through-the-years/z1EU28H93jMh6wfdIcjzbJ/

17. Automotivehalloffame.org. "Warren E. Avis." Retrieved from https://www.automo tivehalloffame.org/honoree/warren-e-avis/

18. Stanleysteemer.com. "The Story of Stanley Steemer." Retrieved from https://www.stanleysteemer.com/about/our-story

19. *Caller Times* (June 19, 2019); stories.whataburger.com

20. O'Connor, Colleen M. (2001) *Faces of San Diego* (page 38). Chicago: Arcadia. ISBN 0-7385-1876-X. OCLC 49900290

21. Long, T. (November 21, 2019) *El Paso Times.* "Former El Paso Mayor Fred Hervey's business went from soda stand to global Circle K brand." Retrieved from https://www.elpasotimes.com/story/news/2019/11/21/circle-k-soda-stand-global-brand-el-paso/4196838002/

22. Centraltexascremation.com. "Obituary for George William Church Jr." Retrieved from https://www.centraltexascremation.com/obituaries/George-Church/#!/Obituary

23. Fowler, G. (April 29, 1988) *New York Times.* "Obituary: Wallace E. Johnson, Co-Founder Holiday Inns Chain in 1950s." Retrieved from https://www.nytimes.com/1988/04/29/obituaries/wallace-e-johnson-co-founder-of-holiday-inns-chain-in-1950-s.html

24. Franchisopedia.com. "Success story: Charles Kemmons Wilson and Holiday Inn." Retrieved from https://franchisopedia.com/global/franchise-articles/holiday-inn-franchise/

25. Breitegan, J. (August 27, 2024) Elephantleanrning.com. "Colonel Sanders: Rejected 1,009 Times Before Starting KFC." Retrieved from https://www.elephantlearning.com/post/colonel-sanders-rejected-over-one-thousand-times-before-starting-kfc

26. KFC.com. "The KFC Story: Humble Beginnings." Retrieved from https://global.kfc.com/our-history

27. Breitegan, J. (August 27, 2024) Elephantleanrning.com. "Colonel Sanders: Rejected 1,009 Times Before Starting KFC." Retrieved from https://www.elephantlearning.com/post/colonel-sanders-rejected-over-one-thousand-times-before-starting-kfc

28. Hernandez, J. (November 3, 2009) *New York Times.* "Obituary: Troy Smith, Founder of Sonic, Dies at 87." Retrieved from https://www.nytimes.com/2009/11/03/business/03smith.html

29. Findagrave.com. "James McLamore." Retrieved from https://www.findagrave.com/memorial/275104827/james-mclamore Thebkbook.com. (2018) "In Memoriam, Davic Edgerton." Retrieved from https://www.thebkbook.com/stories/in-memoriam-david-edgerton-d-2018

30. Pizza.Fandom.com. "Shakey's Pizza" Retrieved from https://pizza.fandom.com/wiki/Shakey's_Pizza

31. Findagrave.com. "Sherwood David 'Shakey' Johnson." Retrieved from https://www.findagrave.com/memorial/134930805/sherwood-david-johnson

32. ArnelPinedaFans.com. (2008) "Unofficial Biography" Archived March 2, 2008, at the Wayback Machine. Retrieved on March 9, 2008.

33. Honan, W. (May 29, 2000) *New York Times.* "Obituary: Richard Block, 78, Pioneer in Digital Computers." Retrieved from https://www.nytimes.com/2000/05/29/us/richard-bloch-78-pioneer-in-digital-computers.html 95thbg.com. "Henry Wollman Bloch." Retrieved from https://95thbg.com/cms/2020/4/11/henry-bloch

34. Scraapehere.com. (February 12, 2024) "Number of H&R Block locations in the United States in 2024." Retrieved from https://www.scrapehero.com/location-reports/H%26R%20Block-USA/

35. Kroc, R. (1977) *Grinding It Out: The Making of McDonald's.* St. Martin's Griffin, New York.

36. *Ibid*

37. Steinberg, B. (May 7, 2024) *New York Post,* "Here's how many McDonald's there are in the world—and the countries where you won't find one." Retrieved from https://nypost.com/2024/05/07/lifestyle/heres-how-many-mcdonalds-there-are-in-the-world-and-the-countries-where-you-wont-find-one/

38. DigitalCommerce360.com; UNC Kenan-Flagler (September 5, 2022)

39. Sicard, S. (February 9, 2023) "How two WWII vets built Waffle House into an empire." Retrieved from https://www.militarytimes.com/off-duty/military-culture/2023/02/09/how-two-wwii-veterans-built-waffle-house-into-an-empire/

40. Fox, M. (May 31, 2006) *New York Times.* "Obituary: James Conway Sr., 78, a founder of Mister Softee, Dies." Retrieved from https://www.nytimes.com/2006/05/31/nyregion/james-conway-sr-78-a-founder-of-mister-softee-dies.html

41. VANews.gov. (January 9, 2023) "Veteran of The Day: Navy Veteran Jack Taylor." Story retrieved from https ://news.va.gov/114608/veteranoftheday-navy-veteran-jack-taylor

42. Enterprise.com. "Global Franchise Opportunities." Retrieved from https://www.enterprise.com/en/global-franchise-opportunities.html

43. *Chicago Tribune.* (August 10, 2021) "Obituary: Jay A. Pritzker." Retrieved from https://www.chicagotribune.com/1999/01/24/jay-a-pritzker-2/

44. Hyatt.com. "Our History." Retrieved from https://about.hyatt.com/en/hyatthistory.html

45. Mitchell, D. (September 5, 2017) "RetroIndy: Burger Chef was 'incrediburgible'." IndyStar. Retrieved from: https://www.indystar.com/story/news/history/retroindy/2017/09/05/retroindy-burger-chef-incrediburgible/609456001/

46. Oliver, M. (June 20, 2004) *Los Angeles Times.* "Obituary: Al Lapin, 76; Founder of International House of Pancakes, Dies." Retrieved from https://www.latimes.com/archives/la-xpm-2004-jun-20-me-lapin20-story

47. *Hartford Courant.* (March 20, 2022) "Obituary: Jerome Martin Lapin." retrieved from https://www.courant.com/obituaries/jerome-martin-lapin-ct/

48. IHOP.com. "Our Story." Retrieved from https://franchise.ihop.com/en/international/our-story

49. NNDB.com. "Matthew Perkins." Retrieved from https://www.nndb.com/people/087/000205469/

50. *Los Angeles Times.* (June 30, 1985) "Obituary: Morris Mirkin, Founder of Rental Car Company, Dies." Retrieved from https://www.latimes.com/archives/la-xpm-1985-06-30-me-201-story.html

51. Rengers, C. (December 3, 2020) *The Wichita Eagle.* "Obituary: Pizza Hut co-founder Frank Carney, a disciplined business giant, dies at 82." Retrieved from https://www.kansas.com/news/business/biz-columns-blogs/carrie-rengers/article247534320.html

52. Fagan, M. (June 15, 2008) *Lawrence Journal-World.* "Reminiscing with 'Pie-In-The-Sky'." Retrieved from https://www2.ljworld.com/news/2008/jun/15/reminiscing_pie_sky/

53. HistoryOasis.com. "Caleb Bradham: The Founder of Pepsi." Retrieved from https://www.historyoasis.com/post/caleb-bradham

54. Coca-ColaCompany.com. "Our History." Retrieved from https://www.coca-colacompany.com/about-us/history

55. Horatio Alger Association. "James A. Patterson: Horatio Alger Award Recipient, Class of 2002." Retrieved from https://horatioalger.org/members/detail/james-a-patterson/

56. Hockey Hall of Fame. "Mike Ilitch: Builder Category." Retrieved from https://www.hhof.com/induction_archives/ind03ilitch.shtml

57. Brzozowski, C. (July 14, 2008) Dbusiness.com. "Earning His Wings." Retrieved from https://www.dbusiness.com/from-the-magazine/earning-his-wings/

58. Dominos.com. "Company Assets." Retrieved from https://media.dominos.com/assets/files/media-kit.pdf

59. *Los Angeles Times.* (June 25, 2008) "Obituary: Hamburger Chain Founder Lost Controlling Shares in a Poker Game." Retrieved from https://www.latimes.com/archives/la-xpm-2008-jun-25-me-hardee25-story.html

60. Tacobell.com. (March 13, 2019) "Meet The Man behind The Bell®." Retrieved from https://www.tacobell.com/stories/glen-bell

61. woodallscm.com

62. McClellan, D. (May 12, 2007) "Obituary: William Becker, 85; helped begin Motel 6, founded Arizona bank." *Los Angeles Times.* Retrieved from https://www.latimes.com/archives/la-xpm-2007-may-12-me-becker12-story.html

63. Theisen, T. (April 1, 2021) Military.com. "'Bonanza' Star Dan Blocker Fought Communists in the Korean War." Retrieved from https://www.military.com/veteran-jobs/bonanza-star-dan-blocker-fought-communists-korean-war.html   METV.com (September 11, 2019) "Dan 'Hoss' Blocker opened the first Bonanza steakhouse in an old bus station." Retrieved from https://www.metv.com/stories/dan-hoss-blocker-opened-the-first-bonanza-steakhouse-in-an-old-bus-station

64. *Riverside-Brookfield Landmark.* (April 7, 2020) "Obituary: Fred T. Rosati, 102; Co-Founder Rosati's Pizza." Retrieved from https://www.rblandmark.com/2020/04/07/fred-t-rosati-102/

65. Cote, Z. (October 25, 2023) DMagazine.com. "Norman Brinker, The Father of Casual Dining." Retrieved from https://www.dmagazine.com/publications/d-ceo/2023/october/norman-brinker-the-founder-of-casual-dining/

66. *The Virginian-Pilot.* (2013) "Obituary: Lloyd Tilghman Tarbutton." Retrieved from https://www.pilotonline.com/obituaries/lloyd-tilghman-tarbutton-naples-fl/

67. Luppi, K. (March 19, 2012) *The Orange County Register.* "At 78, Del Taco Founder Can Still Bring It." Retrieved from https://www.ocregister.com/2012/03/19/at-78-del-taco-founder-can-still-bring-it/

68. Tucker, J. (February 26, 2024) Nav.com. "The Inspirational Story of the Brothers Who Created Arby's." Retrieved from https://www.nav.com/blog/inspirational-story-brothers-behind-arbys-26195/

69. Dollar Car Rental. "About Dollar Car Rental." Retrieved from https://www.dollar.com/AboutUs/Main.aspx

70. *The Connection.* (January 24, 2017) "Obituary: Ted Allen Isaacson." Retrieved from https://mainstreetmediatn.com/articles/obituaries-robertsoncountyconnection/ted-allen-isaacson-6/

71. *Printing News.* (July 22, 2014) "Kwik Kopy Printing Founder Bud Hadfield Passes Away." Retrieved from https://www.printingnews.com/events/press-release/10255072/iced-international-center-for-entreprenurial-development-kwik-kopy-printing-founder-bud-hadfield-passes-away

72. UFL.edu. "Sonny and Lucille Football Endowment." Retrieved from https://www.uff.ufl.edu/giving-opportunities/007607-sonny-and-lucille-tillman-football-endowment

73. Thomas, R. (1992) *Dave's Way*. Berkely Books, New York

74. kikn.com (April 4, 2022); *Wyoming Business Report* (February 12, 2012)

75. Yahoo.com (November 25, 2013) "Obituary: Marsh Fisher, Co-Founder of Century 21 Real Estate Franchise System, Passes Away at 88." Retrieved from https://finance.yahoo.com/news/marsh-fisher-co-founder-century-155442299.html

76. Century21.com. "Century 21 Company Profile." Retrieved from https://www.century21.com/about-us/about/company-profile

77. Miller, S. (September 18, 2008) *The Wall Street Journal*. "Obituary: Hands-On Restaurateur Built Shoney's on Family-Style Food." Retrieved from https://www.wsj.com/articles/SB122126817873531035

78. Leadersmag.com. "Leading By Example: An Interview with Dave Liniger, Chairman and Co-Founder of RE/MAX." Retrieved from https://www.leadersmag.com/issues/2023.2_Apr/Purpose/LEADERS-Dave-Liniger-REMAX.html

79. Legacy.com. "Obituary: Sam M. Ross." Retrieved from https://www.legacy.com/us/obituaries/commercialappeal/name/sam-ross-obituary?id=14374455

80. Jan-Pro.com. (August 10, 2022) "Jan-Pro Cleaning & Disinfecting's VetConnection Program Offers Franchise Opportunities for Veterans." Retrieved from https://jan-pro.com/huntsville/jan-pro-cleaning-disinfectings-vetconnection-program-offers-franchise-opportunities-for-veterans/

81. SunbeltNetwork.com

6. How To Vet a Franchisor

1. Webfx.com. "40+ Franchise Statistics You'll Want To Know for 2024." Retrieved from https://www.webfx.com/industries/franchises/statistics/

9. Finding the Right Franchise for You

1. Wiseman, E. (2024) Private correspondence

2. Theledger.com. (June 25, 2009) "Working Curves." Exercising Franchises prosper with easygoing workouts." Retrieved from https://www.theledger.com/story/news/2006/05/15/mcchead-working-curves-mcchead/8095333007/

3. Wolfoffranchises.com. "What Happened to Quiznos Subs?" Retrieved from https://wolfoffranchises.com/what-happened-to-quiznos-subs/

ACKNOWLEDGMENTS

To my wife, Nicole, for her patience in losing me to my laptop for almost a year, and for her unwavering support and love through good times and bad.

I want to thank my brother, Mark, for the enormous amount of help he offered me in getting this book started and finished. I had no idea where to begin and he stepped in to show me the path forward, the slog of the middle, and the never-ending ending. Plus the monumental task of citations.

This book never comes to pass without Mark.

To my adult children, Jessica, Kasey, and Brandon, I'm so very proud to be your dad.

To my grandson and little buddy, Lane. You are such a bright light in my life and I'm so very proud of you.

To my business partner, part-time therapist, and dear friend, Craig Laquerre. Thank you for your trust and, most importantly, your undying friendship.

For my business colleague and now close friend, Kregg Kish. VSB would not be what it is today without your skills and help. Your reminders that I hit them where I aim have been invaluable.

To my very good friend, Bill Putnam, for being willing to jump into the first G-FORCE location with no questions asked.

To Vish Munusami and his wife, Melanie. Thank you for putting your trust in me as our very first G-FORCE franchise, leading the way as our company trainer and, most importantly, becoming a cherished part of my life as my "adopted" son and daughter.

To my dear friend (and occasional real estate attorney), Tom Quinn, you have always been an inspiration as a family man and a man of honor.

To my corporate staff at VSB, Jason Sperry, John Kling, Rachel Pitts, Lucy Robinson, Staci Kingery, Kay Richards, and Chris Greenhalgh, you are not only the best of the best at what you do, but you inspire me every day to be a better person. Your friendships mean the world to me. I would be lost without you.

To all the VSB franchise owners and their teams, you make it happen day in and day out with no fanfare. I'm incredibly proud of your accomplishments and excited to see the next stages of your entrepreneurial journeys.

Finally, to my dad, Don Child. You deserved so much better than the way the world treated you. This book is dedicated to your memory.

Don Child, WWII Navy Veteran

www.ingramcontent.com/pod-product-compliance
Lightning Source LLC
Chambersburg PA
CBHW030511210326
41597CB00013B/868

A must-read for every veteran considering a franchise

☑ **Discover the franchise world from an insider's perspective**
☑ **Explore the Good, the Bad and the Ugly of franchising**
☑ **Gain valuable lessons to help you choose the right franchise**

"I wish I had this book before signing my franchise agreement. It would've sav[ed] me hundreds of thousands [of dollars], and years of frustration. Every veter[an] considering franchising needs to read this first."
– STEVE LEBLANC, Major, USAF (Retired) & Franchise Owner

"This is the best book I know of to help Veterans wisely consider a franch[ise] business opportunity for their next chapter in life!"
– DOUGLAS A. DWYER, President & CSO, DreamMaker® Bath & Kitchen, a Found[ing] member of VetFran since 1991

"As a veteran with over 20 years in franchising, I've seen too many vets make t[he] wrong moves or get taken advantage of when starting a business. That's wh[y I] respect Jack: he is a passionate advocate for veterans. This book is an hone[st,] practical guide that gives vets the tools to avoid pitfalls and make smart, ethi[cal] decisions. I'm proud to have contributed a chapter and to endorse this muc[h] needed resource."
– JIMMY WEEKS, USAF Veteran, Founder,
Internet Strategy Labs Member, VetFran Committee

"Leave it to a pilot and flight instructor to create a thorough and surprisin[gly] engaging checklist and reference manual for franchisees. Packed with invalua[ble] insights, this book is a fantastic read for anyone considering a franchise and [an] essential resource for veterans. The chapter on responsible franchising stands o[ut] and the appendix of quick checklists is a game-changer for prospective owners.[”]
– SCHUYLER 'ROCKY' REIDEL, Managing Franchise Attorney, Reidel Law Firm

About the Author

Jack has worn many uniforms over the years—gas station attend[ant,] Army soldier, ROTC cadet, Air Force officer and instructor pilot. He l[ater] served as a labor leader and airline captain before turning his focu[s to] entrepreneurship. Today, Jack is a multi-brand franchisor, husb[and,] father, pop-pop, dog dad, brother, funcle, and unapologetic foo[die] (albeit with the palette of a five year old). If this book helps [one] veteran avoid making a costly franchise mistake, he will consider [it a] success.

Jack Child

Book@VeteransInFranchising.com

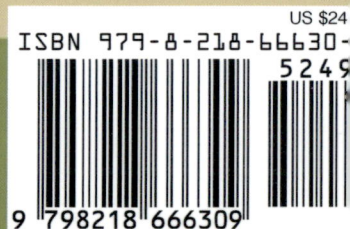

US $24
ISBN 979-8-218-66630-[9]
5249
9 798218 666309

#1 INTERNATIONAL BESTSELLER

THE

24/7

SOLUTION

Proven Strategies for Home Care Business Leaders

EMILY ISBELL

Foreword by JJ Sorrenti, CEO of Best Life Brands